M000266972

TRANSFORMATION MEDITATION

HOME-STUDY TEACHER TRAINING

by Sherrie Wade, M.A.
Licensed Mental Health Counselor (#MH3015)
National Certified Counselor

Teacher Training Manuals include:

- **Teacher Training Instruction Manual:** Theory, practice along with current research on meditation, and comparison of popular techniques. The application of meditation practice along with lesson plans and marketing strategies.

- **Handouts and Samples Manual:** Handouts for the five-class series for foundation and intermediate level courses, and samples of marketing materials.

The Home-Study Teacher Training Course also includes:

- **Two Audio Recordings** (CDs or mp3):
  1. Teacher Training CD: Instructions for teaching the Transformation Meditation Foundation and Intermediate Series.
  2. Infinite Peace CD: Breathing techniques, guided meditations and progressive deep relaxation.

- **Certificate of Achievement:** upon completion of 50-question multiple-choice quiz. The quiz can be taken online using the link provided in your welcome letter.

- **Website Listing** in our **Worldwide Meditation Teachers and Centers Directory** with your name, address, email, phone and link to your website. (6 months free)

- **Email Support** from Sherrie Wade for all registered students.

If you have purchased this book but have not registered for the Teacher Training Course you can register online at **www.transformationmeditation.com**.

This course is suitable for doctors, nurses, social workers, mental health counselors, psychologists, and other health care professionals or yoga and wellness instructors. It is for anyone who wants to learn meditation theory and practice, yoga philosophy, and instructional skills to enhance their personal or professional abilities. Continuing education credits are available from the National Board of Certified Counselors.

Published by
Transformation Meditation, Inc.
Boca Raton, Florida, USA

Transformation Meditation Teacher Training Manuals

First Edition 2000
Second Edition 2005
Third Edition 2012
Fourth Edition 2015

ISBN 978-0-9912686-2-7

Copyright © 2015 Sherrie Wade

All rights reserved

No part of these manuals or recordings may be reproduced, stored in retrieval systems, or transmitted in any form, or by any means, electronic,mechanical, photocopying, recording or otherwise, without prior permission in writing from the publisher.

Those who have registered for and completed the Meditation Home-Study Teacher Training are given permission to copy any of the materials in these manuals for their use in teaching Transformation Meditation as long as our website address is reference in their writing.

For more information, to contact the author,
or to order additional copies, please contact us at:

Transformation Meditation
web: www.TransformationMeditation.com
email: info@TransformationMeditation.com

ACKNOWLEDGEMENTS

I greatly appreciate Swami Shyam for his unprecedented and inspiring interpretations of the ancient texts as well as his tireless love, support and mentoring over the past fifteen years.

Many thanks to my husband, Alan Wade, for his many years of love, support and advice, and to all the friends and family who supported me in this project.

The manual cover photo is of the Beas River in the Himalayan Mountains of India. It represents the flowing river water that constantly moves toward its source, the ocean. When one reaches the source, Pure Consciousness, one realizes one's true potential, which is vast and free like the ocean.

Cover photo:	Gisela Janowski
Cover design:	Stephen Aitken
Photo of author:	Eric Myhr
Editing:	Glen Kezwer
Proofreading:	Karen Jasper
Data entry:	Barbara Burgess
Recording/music:	Alan Wade
Book design:	Eric Myhr, Shelley Astrof

TRANSFORMATION MEDITATION

Teacher Training Instruction Manual

Sherrie Wade

TABLE OF CONTENTS

INTRODUCTION

Congratulations on your interest in teaching Transformation Meditation! Meditation has been shown to be a highly effective and beneficial method for the treatment of numerous psychological and physiological conditions, as well as for improving the overall quality of one's life. As health care professionals, you are striving to do your best to care for your patients, clients or students by using the most efficacious and successful methods. As there is a great demand for qualified meditation instructors, completing this course will be of great benefit to you by increasing and improving your professional skills.

Upon completing this course, you will have the knowledge and lesson plans to enable you to teach meditation privately to your patients or group, and to conduct a Transformation Meditation Course at a clinic, center, school or hospital. You will also improve and deepen your own meditation practice by learning these methods and sharing them with others. As stress is a common denominator contributing to many illnesses, both physical and psychological, you will be learning many methods used to reduce stress and to avoid or heal many stress-related conditions. You will also be helping people to learn how to live a more peaceful and fulfilled life, while realizing their fullest potential. The techniques you share with them will be theirs to use throughout their lifetime; they will continue to receive the benefits even after meeting with you. As we all know, knowledge gained through education is the best prevention for future problems.

Many forms and methods of meditation are being utilized today. Transformation Meditation is an easily applicable form of meditation that brings about rapid results. It is based on the ancient philosophy and science of yoga called *dhyaan yog* [1] or the yoga (union) brought about through meditation. It includes a complete understanding of how the mind and the meditative process

---

1. The transliteration of the Sanskrit terms used in this course is adapted from Feinstein (1999). This system of transliteration allows a more exact pronunciation of these terms. (See the key to Sanskrit pronunciation on page 105.)

work. With this complete knowledge, one's practice is deepened and the results are accelerated. The other well-known and highly practiced form of yoga called Hatha Yoga is based on a system of physical exercises and can be used to prepare one to be able to sit comfortably for meditation. Hatha Yoga exercises are not necessary for this system, but can be recommended as an adjunct to meditation; they are especially helpful to people who have trouble sitting because of tension or pain in their bodies. Other techniques, such as breathing, deep relaxation and constructive thinking, also allow the body to become more relaxed and easy and assist in meditation. These methods will also be covered in this course.

The information in this course is derived from the ancient sources of the philosophy and practice of meditation, including *Patanjali Yog Darshan* and the *Bhagavad Gita.* These great works, although originally written in the East, contain universal truths regarding the practice of meditation and realization of one's highest potential. The original Sanskrit texts were translated and commented on in English by many great authors and meditation masters. This explanation of these ancient works has revealed an unprecedented formula to understand and apply these sometimes confusing and complicated teachings in an easily comprehensible and efficacious framework. These teachings give the answers to many of the questions that each human being must tackle. They show the way to live a healthy, productive and happy life by reducing the anxiety, conflict, depression and stress that many of life's situations can bring about. The works of Swami Shyam, Deepak Chopra, Herbert Benson, Joan Borysenko, Jon Kabat-Zinn, Dean Ornish and other prominent leaders in the field of meditation research and practice have been utilized in formulating this system.

These teachings have been organized into a system called Transformation Meditation. The Transformation Meditation Foundation Series consists of five classes and has been conducted with great success for the past fifteen years. This five-class format will enable you to teach this science very effectively. Included in this home-study course are two manuals and two audio recordings. The first manual consists of: background philosophy, theory and application of all the techniques, relevant scientific research, and outline for each class in the Transformation Meditation Foundation Series and Intermediate Series with instructions and suggestions for teaching. Also included is information on how to market and promote your services in this field, a glossary of the terms used and a list of references. There is some repetition in the chapters that describe the theory of meditation (chapters 1-8, 14 and 15) so that each chapter can also be given to your students as a hand-out pertaining to the subject you are covering, and then discussed with them in the class.

The second manual is a sample handbook consisting of: a Handouts Manual for the Transformation Meditation Foundation Series and for the Intermediate Series (you can adapt this to your needs and give this to your students), with charts and a description of each technique to enable them to practice at home. Also in the second manual is a marketing manual consisting of: letters, press releases, a brochure, common questions and answers sheet, and over a year of a monthly newspaper column with questions and answers.

The first audio recording, *Transformation Meditation Teacher Training*, gives you step-by-step guidance on how to teach the Transformation Meditation Foundation and Intermediate Courses, and help in how to guide your students in meditation practice. The second audio recording, *Infinite Peace,* is a meditation and deep relaxation recording that can help you to learn how to guide these techniques., Copies can also be purchased to sell to your students for their at-home practice. The quiz enclosed will test you on the information you have read and you will receive a Certificate of Achievement and CEUs (where applicable).

CHAPTER 1

TRANSFORMATION MEDITATION IS MORE THAN YOU THINK!

A common reaction from people when I mention meditation is: I have tried to meditate but I can't because I have too many thoughts in my mind. This reaction shows a general misconception about what meditation is. The purpose of the mind is to think. You wouldn't want to change the functioning of the eyes from seeing or the functioning of the ears from hearing, so why try to stop the mind from thinking? The types of thoughts or how many thoughts you have in your mind while you are meditating are not a problem. You don't need to try to control these thoughts. Controlling thoughts or controlling your mind is impossible, as thoughts just seem to appear from nowhere. If I say to you right now, "Don't think of white elephants," the first thought you have will be of white elephants. You see, you can't stop your thoughts from coming by telling yourself not to think them. You can, however, tune in to the space of meditation if you place your attention between or behind the thoughts. If you think, "I am meditating," between "I" and "am" is space and between "am" and "meditating" is also space. You become aware that this space is like the canvas or background on which the thought appears. A painting is painted on a canvas. The canvas is always there behind the paint as the space is there behind the thought.

In yogic theory, from which Transformation Meditation was developed, the mind is considered to be a field of consciousness. Thoughts are called *vrittis* or waves of perception. They come into the mind as if from nowhere or from pure space or consciousness. Thought is nothing but a modification of the space itself that now appears as a thought or a wave of perception on the canvas of your mind. Science tells us that physical forms are not really solid. They are a group of molecules or atoms moving in space. Deepak Chopra (1993), the famous Ayurvedic physician and author, states that even our physical bodies are 99.9% space. Thoughts are also space or Pure Consciousness that appear as waves in the field of the mind. When ice is heated it melts into water and when water is heated it becomes steam, yet it is still H_2O. Just as the frozen water appears as ice and when heated becomes water and then steam, so

5

thoughts move through the body (brain) or mind and, subsiding, return to their source or Pure Consciousness. Using this analogy, the physical body is to ice as thoughts are to water and consciousness is to steam. In essence they are the same substance.

This system of meditation is called Transformation Meditation because the individual waking state of consciousness is transformed into a higher state of awareness. The mental, or thinking, state is transformed back into its originality of pure space or consciousness. In the deep sleep state you are free from troubles, concerns, worries, agitation and even physical pains. When you wake up, as soon as you say, "I am awake," your mind and thoughts come in and the problems return.

There exists a higher state of consciousness where even while awake you can remain at ease and at peace. You can wake up from the waking state of consciousness into the state of higher consciousness. This state is dear to all of us. It is nothing strange to you. You have been in this state any time you have felt easy, peaceful, in love or in harmony with nature. If you can remember these moments, you realize that this potential is there with you all the time.

Remember when you were in a good mood? Then things didn't seem to affect you in the same way. Troubling situations may have arisen but you didn't seem bothered by them. In this higher state of consciousness you are not suppressing your feelings. You still have a full range of emotions; however, you do not become devastated or react as severely to things that are not in your control. You still have thoughts and feelings; however, you are aware that you are more than your thoughts and feelings and you are not limited by them. You are the Knower or observer of your thoughts.

While meditating, you tune in to yourself as the Knower of the mind and thoughts. Changing the thoughts once they have arisen, or trying to think more positively, although useful for developing a more positive approach to life, is only part of this practice. It would be impossible to change the thousands of thoughts that come into your mind every day. However, you as the watcher or Knower can watch these thoughts or waves of perception. The waves of the ocean are nothing but the same ocean water; we call them waves, but they are still ocean water. You do not have to see your thoughts as anything separate from the ocean of your consciousness. They do not have power over You, the Knower, unless you choose to give them your attention or become mixed or identified with them and begin to treat them as real or important. With the practice of Transformation Meditation you develop a great power to transform the way your thinking mechanism works. You are no longer a victim of your mind and thought process. You become free from the problematic or stressful state and experience a higher state of consciousness. You can easily become aware of this higher state of consciousness because it is inherent in you, at the very source of all your thinking.

There are currently over two hundred and fifty psycho-therapeutic theories and numerous self-help strategies and personal growth seminars. In order to find the secrets to successful living we must first examine the lives of people who have practiced a system that resulted in this success and who lived a balanced life. I have observed through my study of Eastern philosophy and, more specifically, yogic science and psychology, that an optimum, healthy psychological state has been obtained by its practitioners.

The yogic system of meditation was first recorded by the sage Patanjali in the fourteenth century B.C. The methods in this work of Patanjali have been shown to be effective through centuries of practice. The result of the practice of meditation is that one achieves a superior state of physical health and psychological well being. There have been numerous interpretations of these ancient teachings that describe this philosophy. Some of them can be confusing and not easily adaptable to modern-day living. Out of that confusion many misconceptions have developed about meditation practice. Transformation Meditation is a scientific approach that clarifies these Eastern teachings and allows one to experience the benefits of meditation quickly and easily.

CHAPTER 2

WHY DO YOU SUFFER?
THE ESSENTIAL PURPOSE OF HUMAN LIFE

There is an old story that portrays how the mind works to bring about suffering. Two young men decided to travel from India to America to gain financial success. After one year in America, one of the men established himself in a lucrative position, married and became financially successful. The other young man met with misfortune and became ill and died. The first young man met someone who was returning to India and asked him to please relay the message to both families regarding his success and his friend's misfortune. The messenger returned to India and relayed the messages. However, he mixed up the names, reporting to one set of parents that their son had died when, in fact, he had married and become financially successful. To the other family, he reported that their son had become rich and married when, in fact, he had met with great misfortune and had died. The parents of the son who died, but were told that he had become successful, celebrated and rejoiced with the news. The family of the son who actually became successful, but were told that he had died, began to mourn with intense grief.

This story portrays how the mind functions. It becomes identified with the thought of either death or happiness and wealth, believes it to be the truth, and either suffers or rejoices. How many times have you suffered needlessly after hearing the wrong information? Have you experienced a misfortune or difficult situation that turned out in the long run to be beneficial for you in some way? Maybe you learned from it or grew from the experience, or it was a warning sign that helped you to avoid a dangerous situation in the future. Your mind has been unskillfully trained through the development of concepts and belief systems to experience all situations according to past experiences. It is limited by these concepts and unable to see the whole picture or complete truth. A blind man touching only the trunk of an elephant would conclude that an elephant is long and thin.

Babies in the womb, with all their needs totally taken care of, are completely connected and at one with their mother. The result is that no fear of separation or sense of duality can arise for them. However, as soon as birth takes place and the umbilical cord is cut, separation is experienced. At that time, due to this new dualistic perspective, fear and pain begin. The infant, whose essence was Pure Consciousness, without thoughts, beliefs and concepts, was experiencing Oneness with everything. Then, at birth or some time soon after, they become a separate person. This is a necessary step in development. Children have to begin to view themselves as separate people, develop independence and learn to take care of themselves. So what goes wrong at this point? Children, in the process of developing their own ego or sense of individuality, forget the experience of Pure Consciousness or their essential nature of Oneness with everything. The idea, then, is not to change this necessary developmental process, but to be able to develop as a fully functioning, independent person and simultaneously experience one's essential nature. The quality of this Pure Consciousness state, or essential nature, is a sense of ease and peacefulness.

When you look at new-born babies, you never think they are bad or anything less then perfect expressions of life. Why, then, do people judge or criticize themselves or others? It is the faulty mechanism or ineffective training that has created the problem, not the innocent, perfect expression of life that was brought into this world some years before. We need to remember this and treat the faulty mechanism, not blame the person or ourselves.

Patanajli Yog Darshan (Shyam, 2001) states that all pain and suffering are due to ignorance of the Self. Modern psychology, a science still comparatively in its infancy, suggests that they are due to one's genetic makeup, childhood experiences, parental influences or learned behaviors and thinking processes. Patanjali takes us to the source of the problem. He answers the question: What is the mechanism in a human being that causes the destructive genetics patterns, harmful parenting and improper thinking? As we know, many people who were brought up in the most abusive environments have risen above their situations and gone on to excel in life. What is different about these individuals and those who continue their self-defeating patterns? We can't continue to blame our parents or their parents or even the proverbial Adam and Eve. We have to take responsibility and learn how the faulty mechanisms of the mind and nervous system work. As soon as you train the mechanism of the mind and strengthen the nervous system through the practice of meditation, you will experience what is called the fourth state of consciousness, or knowledge of the Self. The workings of this human system are then transformed.

The essential purpose of human life, according to the yogic system, is to become aware of, or to realize, one's own true nature. The term "to realize" is used because this is not something that one needs to find, discover or create. Instead, it is the very essence of who we all are. We therefore realize what already exists. It is only because one has shifted their attention away from the experience of their essential nature of Pure Consciousness towards the body, mind, and emotions that they are then not aware of this realized state. Most people experience life in an identified state of consciousness called the waking state. They forget that they exist as the Knower of the experience. When one is aware of oneself as the very life force, or Knower, one is not identifying as only the changing thoughts and feelings. One is in touch with the life itself and experiences the bliss of the very life or higher Self. This explains why one person on vacation, or out in a peaceful natural setting, remains troubled or agitated while another person in the same setting, or even in a busy city, remains peaceful. This shows that it is not the setting or experience, rather it is the condition of the mind that determines the quality of our experience.

Most people are striving for happiness, peace, contentment and freedom from pain and suffering. This state of true peace or happiness is our essential nature; it cannot be found outside of us. The existential questions, such as: Who am I? and What is my purpose? are all answered when one experiences their true nature. This state is what Abraham Maslow (1970) calls a peak or transcendent experience. He indicates that his findings show that everyone has had or can have a peak experience. This experience is not necessarily a consequence of any religious belief or particular denomination, as those from all groups have such experiences.

This experience, according to Maslow (1970), can be scientifically tested. In fact, he states that in interviews "non theistic" people said that they had more religious or transcendent experiences than conventionally religious people. This "peak experience" may initially last for only a few seconds or minutes; however, it is a state filled with knowledge and is also often referred to in yogic science as the "question-less" state. As soon as one brings the attention to the Knower of any experience this peak experience occurs, as one has transcended the mind. This can be accomplished even at the beginning stages of meditation.

One might ask, if everyone is striving for happiness, why is it that some people rob banks, kill other people, and commit acts that seem harmful to themselves and others? No matter what action a person is taking, they ultimately believe it will bring them happiness. Even when someone kills another human being, they do it because they believe, incorrectly of course, that they will feel better. Although these acts might bring moments of relief, they do not bring long term satisfaction. Instead, they create more pain and suffering.

What most people incorrectly believe will bring them happiness is the fulfillment of a desire. It is very tiring to manipulate, and impossible to have, everything the way you desire it all the time, the very nature of life being a state of constant change. When one desires something and then attains it, there is a sense of momentary happiness or fulfillment. As a result, a mistaken belief is developed that if all the desires are met, one will have a happy life. If you analyze your own life and that of others, you can become aware that this is a false belief. For no matter how many desires one fulfills, another one is waiting just around the corner. Yet, there exists for many people the false belief that more money, success, power, love, etc., will bring total happiness and satisfaction. Therefore, most people in their striving for happiness keep living out their desires. When a desire is met they are happy; when a desire is not met they suffer. Fulfilling our desires, although necessary for life, will never bring lasting happiness or peace. In fact, it is the very need to have the things one desires that prevents this. When you get what you want and feel momentarily happy, you then fear its loss if you believe that is what brought your happiness.

This can be seen with the addictive personality which desires the substance, feels good for a while after getting it and then suffers again, needing more when the effect is gone. This addictive behavior applies not only to substances but to people, things, power, money, love, work, etc. Every human being, however, is born with desires, and it is through these desires that one manifests one's life. If one does not seek happiness through fulfilling desires, how will one function in life and achieve happiness? If you follow a desire to its source, through the practice of meditation, you can become aware that behind or between the very thoughts that make up the desire is a state of Pure Consciousness or peace. The desire, then, is seen as a passing wave of perception, and one has the choice to act on it or not. As Shyam (1985) expresses:

> The technique is simply to sit still, watch the space and acquaint yourself with your own Self, the pure Knower. Once you have attained this, you have gained the mastery of controlling desires, which means that any time you want to formulate a desire, just do it, and when you want to dismantle it, just do that. If you want to execute a desire, then release the ability from within yourself and fulfill that desire. If you want to experience pain or bondage, then you are free to create that also. But since you have mastery or you are the master, then everything is just your own form and you are forever the blissful Lord, the Master.

When the mind no longer identifies itself with the problematic waking state of consciousness and experiences Pure Consciousness, one becomes the master rather than the victim of one's own mental and emotional functioning. Regardless of one's dysfunctional childhood or life experience, one can transform the workings of the mind and learn to disengage from mistaken beliefs, desires and concepts that lead to pain and suffering. Instead, one can enjoy the inner state of peace and live in this state of higher consciousness. The proof is there as this state has been obtained and lived by many Self-realized beings throughout history. From their example, or by having your own experience of this state through the practice of meditation, you can become aware that you, too, can achieve this state of higher consciousness.

Chapter 3

Happiness Lies Within

Modern psychology has helped people become aware of their behavior, subconscious mind, ego strength, etc., but it has only touched the surface of the potential of the individual. Carl Jung (1933) said, "Western developments are only a beginner's attempt compared to what is immemorial in the East." To understand completely what the true cause of unhappiness or suffering is, we need to return to a tradition that is thousands of years old and has been proven to be effective by those who have practiced it. When using the scientific method, one performs experiments and reports the results. Practitioners of Eastern psychology and meditation for centuries have done these experiments on themselves and the results have been shown to be truly scientific as they are valid and replicable. Whenever these techniques are practiced, the desired results are obtained and the same results will be accomplished any time the experiment is replicated. Just as the formula H_2O will always make water, meditation practice will result in this higher state of consciousness or knowing one's true nature. When you do this research on your own mind and begin the practice of meditation, you will come to understand the workings of your own mind-mechanism. By meditating on the Knower of your mind, you will directly experience the meditative state.

According to the science of meditation, originated by Sage Patanjali (Shyam, 2001) there are four types of pain and suffering that the human being experiences due to his actions. (I will be using the Sanskrit terms and defining them in English. You may like to familiarize yourself with these terms as often there is not an exact corresponding term in English.) The first type of pain, due to one's action, is called *parinaam dukh.* This is when something is enjoyable but later on results in pain: for example, you overeat an assortment of wonderful foods and then right after eating you experience indigestion and reach for, "plop plop, fizz fizz, oh what a relief it is." The second type of pain, *sanskaar dukh,* is caused by the memory of something that you had but no longer have, such as when you end a relationship or lose a loved one. The third type of pain, or *taap dukh,* comes when your sense of happiness is based on having something that you enjoy but fear to lose, such as owning a beautiful home but worrying that you may lose your job and not be able to afford it. Also, when you are dependent on a relationship as the source of your happiness, you may fear being left alone. The fourth type of pain is due to an imbalance in your energy which may be caused by overwork, overplay, poor diet, sickness or keeping bad company. This type of pain is apparent when you feel tired or are in physical pain and you must get up and go to work.

The past pain is gone and we can't do anything to change the past. The present pain is already here, so it is too late to change that. The future pain can, however, be avoided. How does one avoid that future pain? There is a cute anecdote that my meditation teacher once told on this topic. He said that if you have soft feet and a thorn pricks you, you will feel the pain. You can't help that your feet are soft or that you have already stepped on the thorn, but next time you can wear shoes and that will avoid future pain. To avoid future pain, therefore, you need to have a strong "shoe" covering your mind, as your mind creates the pain. That shoe is the mantra that he suggests: *Amaram Hum, Madhuram Hum.* Its meaning, I am immortal, I am blissful, frees you from the sense of loss and tunes you in to your essential nature, the energy or life, which doesn't change. Then you experience your blissful nature. (The use of mantra will be explained in greater detail later on in the manual.)

Utilizing this mantra, you are able to transcend the waking state functioning of the mind where pain and suffering exist. When you are in deep sleep, pain, emotional or physical, is not experienced but you still exist. Why don't you feel pain? It is because the mind is not active. When you use the mantra, like a shoe that covers your foot, the mantra covers or fills your mind. Then the true Self which is unchanging, free and filled with knowledge is experienced. The thoughts and feelings are then seen to affect only your body and mind, but not the total You. Therefore, when some action is needed to remove pain from the body, and you get a signal of pain, you will take care of it; for example you will remove a thorn that is hurting your foot. At the same time, you can remain free from the effects of any fearful thoughts that the mind may create in relation to it, such as: "Will this thorn hurt me tonight?" or "Will it get infected?" These thoughts may be necessary for some action to be taken, but if you dwell on them or identify with them you will remain fearful. Through this technique, one can stay free from the effects of these disturbing thoughts. Even though the body and mind may react, you, the Knower of the thoughts, can observe those thoughts as passing waves of perception; some require action and some do not.

The Tenth Man

There is an old story about ten men who set sail on a long journey out to sea. After many days of sailing in rough seas, they arrive back at the shore. They takes turns counting the other men and, forgetting to count themselves, conclude that there are nine men who have successfully made the trip. They began to weep and cry as they truly believe that the tenth man has drowned. When a passerby comes and sees their grief, he counts ten men and points out to them their mistake of forgetting to count themselves.

This story represents what is known to be the real cause of all suffering. Inside our own being is a well of peace and happiness. Whenever one's joy is based exclusively on the experiences in life and one's true Self is forgotten, suffering occurs. Through the practice of meditation, one becomes aware of one's source or true Self. The experience of the Self is Pure Existence, Pure Consciousness and Bliss. This is available to every breathing, thinking human being. It has often been said that happiness lies within. Through meditation practice, you return to your source of happiness which is you. Then, by remembering your Self, you have the power to deal with all the changing situations in your life. This happiness no one can ever take away from you because it is you.

A man searched high and low for his glasses. Filled with frustration and irritation, he turned to his wife asking for help. She said to him, "Dear, they are right there on your eyes." Happiness and freedom from suffering are right there within you. It always has been and always will be.

A Lesson in True Happiness

It was pouring rain outside one day when I was in India. My apartment was a four-block walk from the meditation institute where I was studying. I put on my rain gear and decided to make my way down to the meditation hall. This entailed putting on my boots which were only ankle high, a bulky rain poncho, which felt very awkward, and carrying an umbrella. I then made my way down the three flights of dirt stairs which by this time were mostly mud. I lived up the side of a steep mountain and had to walk down to reach the road. After walking one block on the road, which had became a flowing river, I had to cross the gully. During heavy rain the gully becomes like a rushing river as the flood waters come down from the top of the mountains.

Having only ankle-high boots, I decided to walk back up the side of the mountain where I could cross over on some rocks rather then wading through knee-deep water. If you are at all familiar with India you will know that the sewer system empties onto the road, so this wasn't only pure mud that I was walking in. I managed to climb up the mountain and cross the gully, getting wet only above my ankles, then back down onto the road where the passing trucks and busses sprayed me with mud.

I finally made it to the meditation hall drenched from head to toe. I took off my rain gear, feeling relieved to be seated in the hall and drying off. I breathed a sigh knowing that I could stay parked here all day and maybe by nighttime it would have stopped raining. I waited patiently and meditated in the hall for about fifteen minutes, and then Swami-ji, my meditation teacher, arrived.

He walked into the room declaring that it was a beautiful day and we should all take a walk down to the Traveler's Lodge, a hotel about two blocks past where I had just come from (back across the gully) and conduct the session there. I couldn't believe what I was hearing. I was just drying off and becoming comfortable and he was suggesting going back out in the rain. My mind raced through all sorts of thoughts, from "I'm staying right here" to "I have to find a taxi to drive me back." The idea of walking back in the rain was preposterous. I didn't want to stay in the hall by myself and miss that day's session, so I got up and walked outside with everyone. Swami-ji was so full of joy, just like a little kid going out to play in the rain or snow. Somehow I got caught up in all the excitement and started walking back down the road. Rather then trying to avoid the gully, we just walked right through the knee-deep water, singing and playing in the rain. When we got to the Travelers Lodge, I was so happy that my wet feet didn't even bother me. In fact, my wool socks seemed to keep my feet warm and I became quite comfortable.

Reflecting on this later, I became aware of what a truly happy state is. I observed that Swami-ji didn't conclude there was something wrong with the rain. He was able to just flow in the moment and truly enjoy whatever life was giving him. Through the practice of meditation one de-identifies with thoughts that create uneasiness. I learned through this experience that if I free myself from my conditioned thoughts and the desire to have things meet my preference, then life can be enjoyed to the fullest, regardless of the external environment or circumstances.

CHAPTER 4

JUST LET IT GO ALREADY!
THE SCIENCE OF THE MIND

Doesn't it irritate you when you are suffering because of a particular situation and someone says to you, "Just let it go already"? Why is it so difficult to just let go of negative thoughts and emotions, or thoughts about situations that you are unable to change? We all know that our thoughts and feelings create the experience of our life. Then why can't we choose to think positively and let go of these disturbing, irrational fears, worries and agitation?

If a two-hundred-pound weight was placed in front of you, it would be impossible for you to lift it over your head without the proper training. You would have to train your muscles and increase your stamina. This would require lifting weights of various pounds every day over time, increasing the weight as you progress; then, eventually, you would be able to lift it. Just as you need to understand the theory of weight lifting, you need to understand how the mind works in order to let go of disturbing thoughts and feelings.

According to the science of meditation, the mind is considered the instrument that the Self uses for perception. The mind has four functions or aspects. The lower mind is called *manas* in Sanskrit; it is the part which collects incoming data. To utilize this information intelligently, two other functions of the mind come into operation. The first is the *ahankaar*, or sense of I-ness; this changes the experience by relating it to the sense of the individual and his own identity. The sensory motor mind can see a flower, but the I-ness says, "I see a flower." When information is presented to the mind, a decision, judgment, or discriminative ability is necessary, and this is called the power of the intellect, or the *buddhi*. The fourth function of the mind is the memory bank, which stores all past experiences; this is called the *chitt*. Beyond the mind and mental functioning lies the inner or higher field of consciousness called the "Self." This is observed through the practice of meditation.

We are born with mental impressions and develop new ones throughout our lifetime. These impressions are called *sanskaars*.

They include one's desires, memories and personality. Unless one begins to awaken the knowledge of their true nature, one will continue to act according to these mental patterns. This explains why someone continues to perform particular actions, such as remaining in an unhealthy relationship or unfulfilling job, even though these actions do not truly bring them what they want.

Sanskaars also include the memory of your name, relations, likes and dislikes; so you cannot eliminate all your *sanskaars*. You can remove the identification with your false beliefs and concepts that your mind has recorded as desires, which it mistakenly thinks it needs in order to be happy. Happiness that is based only on fulfilling a desire later leads to unhappiness, such as when one over-eats or drinks or bases one's satisfaction solely on acquiring material possessions. The mind has created these *sanskaars* because the fulfillment of these desires seems to bring about happiness temporarily. The mind, therefore, continues in the pattern of trying to satisfy all of its desires, mistakenly thinking that this will lead to total happiness and fulfillment.

True happiness is the experience of one's true nature and is not dependent on fulfilling one's desires. The true Self, which is pure, often mistakenly identifies itself as a thought or belief and takes on the quality of that thought or belief, as if it were real. This mixture state is called *sanyog* in Sanskrit. The true Self becomes mixed with the mind and forgets itself, the pure being. One can train the mind to de-identify with thoughts and beliefs that pass through the awareness and create pain and suffering. Through this training one becomes aware of their true nature or the Knower of the thoughts. One then creates new impressions or *sanskaars* that will bring the attention to the true Self which is always shining and is full of peace and joy. Through meditation practice, one can become aware of these *sanskaars* or mistaken beliefs. These *sanskaars* have created grooves or impressions in the mind and one can choose to either act on them, let them go or change them. The power of meditation is that not every negative thought and belief has to be changed, as this would be a tedious and never-ending project; instead, one can observe thoughts as waves of perception. The true Self is not affected by these passing waves of perception.

Ego psychologists believe that dis-identification and non-attachment are contrary, if not impossible, for healthy development. Borderline and other personality disorders are said to have developed from the pre-oedipal separation-individuation state, according to object relations theory. At the separation-individuation state there is not any differentiation between self and other objects. Development of the object-related self is the task at this stage and a requirement for normal development, as cited in Engler (1986). With this in mind, meditation could be seen to be a deterrent to healthy ego development.

Jack Engler, Ph.D. (1986), who was the clinical director of the Schift Psychiatric Hospital and a supervising psychologist on the faculty of Harvard Medical School, is also a Vipassana, "insight," meditator. He points out that in meditation one must see through the illusion of the body/mind self by dis-identifying from the personal identity. He arrived at the view that you have to develop a strong ego before you can dis-identify with it. To do this one must understand exactly what the ego is and how it functions.

In yoga theory the ego is considered to be the sense of "I." When this sense of "I" is either denied or identified with, the problems occur. Therefore, the practice of meditation is not to remove the "ego" or sense of "I" as many might conclude. It also is not meant for one to revert back to a state where there is no attachment to anything, since then one could not function constructively. Through meditation practice, one learns to use the ego, body and mind to their utmost capacity and simultaneously know that the very power for them to function comes from the higher Self. In fact, it is said that for the Self-realized one the ego is so vast that it contains the entire universe, and all are seen as one being, the very same Self. That Self is considered to be who we are and not limited to the individual ego that we must function through.

In the well-known second aphorism of *Patanjali Yog Darshan*, *yogash chitt vritti nirodhah*, Shyam (2001) explains that yoga means union with the higher consciousness. The most subtle aspects of thought is considered to be *vrittis* or waves of perception. Optimum existence is achieved when all the waves of perception, that arise in the field of the mind, are known as the very same Pure

Consciousness in which they appear. Similarly, the waves in the ocean arise and we call them waves, but they are the same ocean water. Through the practice of meditation, one develops the ability of the mind. One is then able to de-identify with the passing waves or thoughts that lead one towards pain or suffering, and instead to focus on the Knower of these thoughts. The Knower is the Pure Consciousness, which is unchanging and always peaceful. When the consciousness which exists behind the thought process, or the Knower, no longer identifies itself with any particular thought and sees all the waves as Pure Consciousness, unity with the Self, or peace, is experienced.

Through the practice of meditation and the observation of one's thoughts, one develops the *buddhi,* or power of discrimination. The mind is seen as an instrument that the Self uses to perceive the world. One develops the power to observe one's mental functioning and becomes the master. The intellect is then said to be purified, as it works to continuously reveal the true being or Self, forever free and pure, unmixed with the thoughts or impressions of the mind.

Some of the key aphorisms of *Patanjali Yog Darshan* are sometimes translated from the original Sanskrit into English in a way that would lead one to think that it is necessary to control or stop the mind. This misunderstanding causes people to have difficulty in meditation. They realize as soon as they close their eyes that the mind is filled with many thoughts. Controlling or stopping these thoughts would be impossible because the nature and function of the mind is to think. What Patanjali is really saying is that the thoughts are nothing more than waves of perception. One can allow them to pass without holding on to them, or one can watch them as if on a movie screen. As one focuses on the consciousness out of which these waves are arising, or the gap or space between the thoughts, one is led to the experience of inner peace. It might then appear as if the thoughts have stopped because you, the Knower of the thoughts, is not engaged in seeing thoughts. Rather, one becomes established in Pure Consciousness, which is the very essence of the thought. Just as a wave is, in essence, the same ocean water but appears as a wave when it arises or moves, so our thoughts are the same Pure Consciousness in motion. With this purified intellect, thoughts are never a problem. They are the same Pure Consciousness now appearing as a passing wave of perception. They are not necessarily true or false or good or bad; they are just perceptions. You can discriminate as to their usefulness.

There are four states of consciousness that the human being experiences: deep sleep, dream, waking, and the fourth—the meditation state. In the waking state one is completely identified with one's thoughts and feelings. Therefore, one's experience of life is based on whatever thoughts or feelings are present at the time. In the fourth state of consciousness one is free from the confines of the body and mind. One transcends the individual waking state of consciousness and experiences the eternal state of peace inside one's own being. When you are dreaming and then wake up, you know that your dream was unreal and illusory. The suffering or happiness in the dream is no longer with you, even though it appeared real while you were dreaming. In the same way, you can also awaken from the waking state into the fourth state, since the waking state is a more conscious state than the dream state, and the fourth state is a more conscious state than the waking state. Through the practice of meditation you can wake up from the waking state and experience the fourth state of higher consciousness which is known as Pure Existence, Consciousness and Bliss, the state free from the problems that occur within the mind.

This phenomenon of taking what is illusion to be real is often referred to as "the snake in the rope." A man is walking down the road and jumps with fear as he sees a "snake." All the physiological symptoms of fear arise: he is sweating, his heart is racing, and his mind and body are preparing to fight or run away. Then, as he approaches more closely, he realizes that it is only a rope. This is often related to the illusory quality of the waking state mind: though it appears to be so real, one comes to see that it must be illusory because it is always changing.

CHAPTER 5

THE SELF-REALIZED PERSON

*Imagine all the people living life in peace. You may say
I'm a dreamer but I'm not the only one. I hope someday
you will join us and the world will live as one.*

We have heard these famous words of John Lennon for three decades now. Could the world really live at peace? Does it make sense to demonstrate against a war, fight in a war or march for peace when you are arguing with your own spouse, children or family members? How can you learn to be peaceful within yourself and with your own family? To achieve this state of peace, one needs to look at someone who has attained this ideal state of optimum psychological health and peacefulness, the Self-realized person. We can learn from them the qualities they possess and how they have achieved them.

When you observe your own mind's functioning, you can become aware of the four states of consciousness: waking state, dream state, deep sleep state, and the higher consciousness or the fourth state. In the deep sleep state you can observe that there is no pain or problem. You are completely at peace regardless of what you might have been experiencing in the waking state or dream state. Yet you have to wake up from sleep or dreaming, and then the pain and problems return. In the fourth state, or higher consciousness state, there is also this sense of freedom from pain and problems; yet, unlike in deep sleep, one is awake and alert. In fact, one is often more alert or even super-conscious. This state is experienced in meditation. It is described in Sanskrit as one's essential nature, *Sat-Chit-Aanand,* Pure Existence, Pure Consciousness and Pure Bliss.

When you become aware of the space behind the thoughts or the gap between the thoughts, what remains is this state of inner peace. It is like looking at a blank canvas. Before the artist paints on it, it is pure white; yet even after the pictures are painted, behind the paint is still always the blank canvas. The canvas of your awareness is the blue-black space behind your closed eyes, and on that canvas or screen appear all of the thoughts. It can also be compared to watching a movie. The movie is projected onto a blank screen; we are unaware of the screen behind the movie images, yet the screen is always there in back of all the projections of light. In the same way, the space is always there behind the projection of the thoughts, images and pictures in your mind.

Many people are searching for peace of mind. They may think it can be obtained by having only peaceful thoughts, or by the absence of any thought. However, the nature of the mind is to generate thoughts and images. Sometimes thoughts are pleasant or peaceful, while other types of thoughts can create agitation, worry, doubt and fear. Therefore, a state of peace cannot always be achieved when you are engaged with your mind's thoughts or with your inner feelings. The notion of total "peace of mind," therefore, is a misnomer. Peace can be experienced when you are in touch with the observer or Knower of the mind, rather than when you are focused only on your thoughts. From that vantage point, one can observe that there are thoughts in the mind, but there is also a blue-black space behind the thoughts and that space is always peaceful. As soon as you close your eyes, this vast space of peace can be seen.

Most people have experienced this fourth state of consciousness, or state of perfect peacefulness, for brief moments. This state has also been termed "Oneness" with the pure Self. Psychologists have called it "a peak experience." Whenever one is in love, or feeling absorbed with the beauty of nature or perfectly peaceful, this Oneness state, or peak, can also be experienced. When this most highly evolved or ultimate psychological state is experienced, and this fourth state of consciousness is lived all the time, it is termed Self-realization. Then it is said that this ideal or optimally healthy and peaceful person has realized their own Self or true nature.

The Self-realized person can live life with total peace and freedom and still fully partake in all aspects of the world. They can remain the Knower or witness self, uninvolved with the changes in the body and mind. They will never view others as separate in terms of their essential nature, as they are tuned in to the very life essence that we all are. They maintain the ability to decide what is most useful and beneficial for them and everyone, as everyone is seen as them. They function as a separate independent person, yet their vision is of the whole. This person still has their personality, likes and dislikes, but is not bound by certain traits, nor are they a victim of their desires.

This inner state of happiness and peace is unchanging, and therefore it can be experienced regardless of the external situation. The body and mind may be affected but the inner being is never hurt. I remember a story told to me by my meditation teacher's daughter. She said that when she was a young girl, she fell off her bicycle and scraped her knee. She came running to her daddy for comfort. He said to her, "Your body is hurt, not you." She was always reminded, even at a young age, that the body or feelings can be hurt but the real Self never gets cut or hurt. This type of training is missing in our culture and society. Most children are taught that they are only individuals, totally separate from others. They are taught that they are their name, physical body and, later, their qualifications. They begin to say, "I am this personality, and I am different and therefore separate from all others." They believe that the body form is who they are; and when the body or emotions are in pain, or when they are dying, they will not have the skills to get free from the fear and pain. Even if the fear or emotional upset is irrational, they will still get caught in it. Therefore, many people are in their own self-imposed prison called the waking state of consciousness.

Transformation Meditation is inherently a psychological theory of optimum existence. It is based on the scientific research done by yoga masters who for thousands of years studied their own system and states of consciousness. It never requires any dogma or religious belief and is amenable to all religions, as it is universal. The ancient Sanskrit scripture, the *Bhagavad Gita*, often read by those practicing Hinduism, also contains the system of yoga, or unity consciousness, which can also be interpreted as an advanced psychological theory containing universal truths.

The Self-realized person is described in the *Bhagavad Gita* (Shyam, 1985). When a person is aware of his true Self, the immortal consciousness, he experiences fearlessness. This consciousness is explained in Chapter Two, Verse 23, as the immortal Self that, "cannot be cut by weapons, burnt by fire, wet by water, or dried by wind, as it is indestructible." To this verse the author adds that the true Self also cannot be hurt by words, as this is a common problem for many people who feel insulted when people criticize or verbally abuse them. This is supplemented so one will have the knowledge that words also cannot hurt the space or Self.

Self-realized people remain in this knowledge of the true Self and have mastery over the senses. Although they use the senses for perceiving the world, they will not be victimized by cravings, desires or addictions. They remain surrendered to their higher Self, not considering their personality self, with its particular concepts, as the doer. Instead, they operate through non-doership, which means that they are in touch with their higher awareness and not only subject to the patterns that have developed through their life experiences. They know that they are pure like the sky space and free. Therefore, someone who had experienced a trauma in childhood or a difficult upbringing would not be limited by that experience. Each moment would be a new beginning, not subject to past beliefs or concepts. One would be free to act according to the present situation rather than forced to react according to past experiences, or illogical or mistaken beliefs and ideas.

The Realized one always acts out of truthfulness, forgiveness and harmlessness, creating harmony by doing that which is best for everyone, seeing everyone as their own Self. They become a master, living in the total freedom of each moment, never bringing in past pain or future expectations, and yet still displaying all the human emotions without being limited by them. They have a full range of emotional responses, but know themselves as the Knower or Self which is always free from being identified with the sensations in their body and the thoughts and beliefs in their mind. They can use the mind as a tool, yet not be bound by it. Even in times of sadness, as when a loved one leaves or passes on, one might be crying, yet simultaneously knowing that one is not limited by these changing emotions. They would have the inner knowledge that the true Self never dies, only the body goes through changes.

Emotions would not be suppressed or necessarily expressed, rather dealt with as appropriate to the situation. Thoughts and emotions would be experienced as passing waves of perception. We need to have these thoughts and emotions to preserve our bodies and live life. One would have to know to leave a burning building or to avoid jumping in a cold river. However, one would not need to maintain the fear and terror when it is no longer necessary to protect the body, as these destructive emotions now begin to weaken it. Just as the waves in the ocean are passing and the calmness is always below the surface, the thoughts and emotions are passing waves and the calmness is always there behind them.

This higher state of consciousness may seem very difficult to obtain. Even though very few people throughout history have reached this completely Self-realized state, we can observe through their example that it is possible and begin the practice. They would say to you that you are already Self-realized, you just need to know it, experience it and remember it all the time. Albert Einstein arrived at the same conclusion in the twentieth century. He said:

> A human being is part of the whole, called by us the universe, a part limited in time and space. He experiences himself, his thoughts, and feelings as something separated from the rest ... a kind of optical delusion of his consciousness.

Through the study and practice of the philosophy of meditation, one can begin to maintain a state of consciousness where this optical delusion is removed and the Oneness of all life is known. Imagine yourself living life in peace. To the Self-realized person the world is of one consciousness and one being, pure and free. When you live from this perspective of peace, you can only create peace in your presence. Through each individual's efforts towards living in this state of peace, the world has no choice but to reflect this highest state of consciousness, which is all peace.

CHAPTER 6

THE ROYAL PATH:
THE EIGHT LIMBS OF YOGA AND THE STAGES OF MEDITATION

The ancient science of yoga is a complete system which works with one's actions, thoughts, feelings, body and spirit to unfold the healthiest and happiest way of life. This system is called *Raj Yog,* the royal path, also known as the eight limbs of yoga. These eight limbs are often described as eight branches of the same tree. They are guidelines which provide a holistic system for one to obtain optimum psychological, spiritual and physical health. Many of the current therapies and scientific findings are confirming what yogic science has documented thousands of years ago. The following is a brief summary of this system. For more information you can refer to the many commentaries that have been written on *Patanjali Yog, Saadhanaa Paad* (Chapter two, Verse 29). One such writing by Shyam (2001) is recommended in the reference section of this manual. You can also refer to the chart on the "Eight Limbs," in your Handouts Manual, for a graphic diagram of this system.

The first limb, *yam,* improves the mind, freeing it from agitation. Certain actions create emotional pain and suffering; not engaging in these actions will create calmness. Calming actions include non-violence, non-deception, non-stealing, and constant acting and thinking towards the realization of the highest Self by conserving one's vital life force energy. Also included in the *yams* is that one should have the awareness of the tendency of the mind to want to possess many unnecessary material things. Material possessions can be a source of great joy, but can also cause suffering when one becomes attached to them. They can sometimes prevent one from living in peace because of the fear of losing them or the struggle to pay for them or take care of them. I remember one of my meditation students who owned several homes, one being a mansion on the oceanfront. She was obviously very wealthy. She came to class one day and said, "I have nowhere to meditate." I looked at her with amazement and said, "How can that be? You live in a mansion!" She said that her staff were always around and that even when she was in the bathroom, unless the shower was running, someone would be knocking on her door to ask her some-thing. This is an example of how acquiring possessions can create the problem of having to take care of them.

The second limb is called *niyam*, injunctions for the purifica-tion of the mind. The mind can be purified in the following ways: By following the laws of proper diet and exercise; by taking everything as it comes and remaining happy through proper thinking; through strenuous living, which refers to a lifestyle whereby one is active and not lethargic; through the study of higher awareness, by con-stantly observing one's mind and reactions to the situations of life, and simultaneously maintaining the awareness of the higher Self; through reading and reflecting on writings that pertain to higher thought; and by devotion to the higher Self, which means rather than being devoted to obtaining happiness only through material possessions and relations, one knows the fulfilled state that comes from remaining aware of the higher Self. Through these methods, one develops the power to concentrate the mind and allow it to re-main fixed on positive, life-supportive thoughts. Many of the cur-rent psychotherapies and psychological theories are also based on these premises. They include becoming aware of negative, irratio-nal beliefs, or cognitive distortions (as in the cognitive therapies). Undesirable thoughts come into the mind because of greed, anger and attachment. There is a variance of the strength or power of these undesirable thoughts. If such thoughts are replaced, these negative tendencies are slowly reduced.

The third limb is *aasan*, which means posture or seat. In vari-ous body therapies, one works with the physical body so that it be-comes free of pain and strain. This limb includes exercise and yoga postures to create a sense of ease in the physical body. Proper diet and nutrition help you to feel healthy, and have a strong nervous system and a responsive immune system. Chemical imbalances in the brain that lead to depression, anxiety and drug addiction can be helped or neutralized. When the body feels more balanced and healthy, it is easier to handle life's difficulties and to sit still to practice relaxation and meditation. Progressive deep relaxation is a technique used by yoga teachers and has also been adapted and used by psychologists. Psychologists use it to create a conditioned response, pairing relaxation with a disturbing event so that the patient experiences calmness rather than fear when dealing with anxiety or phobias. Yoga teachers use it at the end of a yoga class. After the yoga poses are complete, the class is led in a deep relaxation to allow the body and mind to become completely relaxed.

The next limb, *praanaayaam,* is the control of the breath. Breathing techniques regulate one's energies by training the breathing mechanism. The breath is the part of the autonomic nervous system that is both automatically and voluntarily controlled. Breath is closely linked with the emotions. When one is calm, the breath is deep and slow. When one is tense, anxious, angry or fearful the breath is either held or it becomes irregular, short or difficult. Therefore, by changing your breathing pattern you can regulate your emotions and feel calm. These techniques have also been known to strengthen the nervous system and to switch on the parasympathetic part of the autonomic nervous system. By changing one's orientation from a sympathetic, or more active, mode to a parasympathetic mode through breathing techniques, one's nervous system can rest, relax and repair. This switch is imperative when trying to fall asleep.

The technique of diaphragmatic breathing (described more in Chapter 15) moves the diaphragm, pressing it on the lower portion of the lungs and releasing more carbon dioxide as one exhales. There is then room to expand the abdomen on the inhalation to take in a larger supply of fresh oxygen. This oxygen and *praan*, or life force energy, taken in with the breath oxygenates and revitalizes all the cells, organs, glands and the brain. When one is anxious, the lungs fill with carbon dioxide and the introduction of fresh oxygen is difficult. This often occurs during an anxiety or panic attack. The person cannot take in any fresh oxygen and feels as if they cannot breath. With diaphragmatic breathing, one exhales all the stale air, making room to bring in more oxygen. The fresh oxygen then creates a calming effect and strengthens the nervous and immune systems.

The fifth limb, *pratyahaar*, is stability of the mind in itself. By not overindulging the senses through addictive or compulsive eating, drinking, sexual activity, etc., one doesn't deplete the vital energy. In this practice one utilizes their energy, conserving it even more effectively, by turning it inward and focusing on one's higher Self. Meditation is the result; one feels relaxed and easy and the mind becomes calm and focused.

The next three limbs make up what we call meditation. The sixth is *dhaarnaa*, concentration. To begin the practice of meditation one must learn to concentrate by having the mind remain on an object or point in space. The breath, a word, a candle or flower can be used as an object for concentration. A special word or sound, called a mantra, is often used; this creates a vibration of peace and relaxes the mind. The seventh limb, *dhyaan*, is the unbroken concentration on one object. In this type of concentration, your attention is directed to the object of concentration over and over again and then eventually to the Knower of the object. Any thoughts or images that pass through your awareness are not a bother to you as you are not attending to them or pushing them away. This is similar to attending someone you are speaking with and not being aware of the other people in the room. The eighth limb is the outcome of this unbroken concentration. This is termed *samaadhi*, which is the goal of meditation. When one obtains this unbroken concentration, even for a few moments, one transcends the individual awareness. One is then de-identified with the mind and physical body and merges or unites with the space of Pure Consciousness or pure peace.

When one is combining all these approaches, growth is thorough, complete and accelerated. The nature of the mind is that the thoughts or waves of perception and the impressions or grooves that have been ingrained in the mind are unlimited or infinite. Therefore, trying to change them all would be impossible. Through the technique of de-identification, one is trained to not get mixed in any of these thoughts or impressions, and thus it is not always necessary to analyze every thought or experience. The focus in de-identification is on freeing oneself from all distorted and destructive unconscious impressions without having to sort through them all. One becomes the witness or watcher of the mind rather than a victim of it. Then the watcher can watch itself and experience this inner state of peace. These eight limbs taken together are a complete, holistic system to obtaining total health of body, mind and spirit.

The Stages of Meditation *(Samaadhi)*

In *Patanjali Yog Darshan* (Shyam, 2001), Chapter 2, Verses 17-19 explain the various stages that the meditator may experience. The last three limbs of the eight limbs are: concentration, meditation and *samaadhi*, the culmination. *Samaadhi* itself is described as having seven stages. The first stage is inquiry into the objects *(vitark samaadhi)*. In meditation, when one focuses on an object for some time, the name and form of the object is held with unbroken concentration. After more intense concentration, the name and form begin to fade, but the spatial image of the object is still there. This is the second stage called *nirvitark samaadhi* and the former is called *savitark samaadhi*. The same process is apparent when one is focusing on a thought or a mantra. First, the name and meaning of the word are held, and then just a sense of the space of it without name, form and meaning or knowledge of the thought. This third and fourth stage is called *savichaar* and then *nirvichaar samaadhi*. The fifth stage is called *aanand* or bliss. It occurs in meditation when you are permeated by the awareness of bliss and you feel only joy. A runner or athlete may describe a similar state where bliss is experienced and call it the "zone."

It is important not to get fixed in blissful experience in meditation and think that your meditation is now complete, as even at this stage you still remain in the field of change. The sixth stage is called *asmitaa* (I alone). At this stage there is no feeling even of peacefulness or joy. There is just the awareness that "I am." In this stage you are closer to your source which is beyond experience. Then, after some time, the individual mind merges into the whole, or Absolute Pure Existence and knowingness. This seventh stage is called *nirbeej* (without seed) *samaadhi*, where there is no seed or covering to the pure space that you are. (Also refer to the sheet in your Handouts Manual and the teacher training audio recording.)

One of the important things to remember is that the Knower, that you are, is forever You. These stages are just descriptions of the human mind and its functioning to guide you to the realization of the pure being that you are already. Rather than limiting your practice to these stages, you can use them to help you become more observant in your meditation. You can watch the progression of your mind's thoughts when you implement the technique of meditation. Then you can watch as you return your attention to the source of the thoughts. This source is always present, but gets covered over when you became identified with yourself as the very "I" or ego, separate from your source, the purity of being.

Even in the beginning stages of meditation you can have a glimpse of *samaadhi,* which is your true nature, as the light of the true Self is always shining like the sun. The very light or power that is shining on the mind gives it the ability to function. The "you" that was there in deep sleep wakes up in the morning and you may say "I woke up"; but who were you when you were asleep, before you identified yourself as a body and a mind? That "you" which is forever shining is not limited by the advent of an "I" body form. Even in deep sleep your breathing, heart beat and digestion continue. Therefore, you are the "you" that was there prior to becoming the "I" body form. When you know that, you remain aware of your purity and freedom. It is only when you become the "I" that your mind can begin to trouble you. Without the identification with the "I," you are the same blissful being you were the whole time you were in deep sleep. The work, then, is to use the mind and body most effectively and, simultaneously, to know yourself as free from the "I." Then you will remain free from the thoughts in the mind. Someone else's thoughts will not cause you pain. When you are not caught up with your own thoughts, then you also will remain free of accompanying mental and emotional pain which is your own creation due to your thought about it.

Chapter 7

The Obstacles to Self-realization

He who has attained the consciousness of inner happiness enjoys the Bliss of the Absolute and remains aware of his own true nature. He is said to have realized his own Self, the nature of which is all peace. (Bhagavad Gita, 5:24)

Is it the situation, other people, the lack of good company or your physical body that is creating unhappiness? Can you feel peaceful and fulfilled regardless of external circumstances? Although you can't always change what you do not like about your life, can you change your attitude or perspective?

Patanjali (Shyam, 2001) discusses five obstacles called *klaysh.* When these are removed, one obtains the Self-realized state. These obstacles arise in everyone and until they are dissolved one cannot experience true happiness. The first obstacle or *klaysh* is ignorance of the Self, *avidya.* The remaining four are based on this lack of knowledge of the Self. Therefore, this is the most important obstacle. All pain and suffering stem from this one obstacle. Whenever you believe that permanent happiness comes only through material possessions, relationships, gaining power, worldly success, or your physical health or attributes, you are living in ignorance. It is only when one realizes or comes to know the Self, which is where permanent happiness comes from, that one is freed from this ignorance.

If you were to believe only what your senses tell you, you would believe that the world is flat and stationary. In the same way, if you believe only what your mind is telling you, you will be a victim to sensory pleasures. You will remain in ignorance as you will not know the true Self, which is inherently pleasing. When the true Self, due to the influence of *avidya klaysh,* or ignorance, mixes with the thoughts in the mind, one forgets the pure awareness or the real Self. Just as when water and sugar are mixed you cannot see the sugar, in the same way in this mixture state you are not aware of the true Self. The mind or individual personality is super-imposed on the Self and becomes totally mixed with it. Therefore, *avidyaa*, or ignorance, of the Self is the ground from where all the other obsticles arise.

The second obstacle is called *asmitaa*, which is the thought "I am separate from the Self." This is when one believes whatever thought or feeling passes in the mind or body to be the truth. When one thinks that one is only the body and mind, one believes one is separate from the Self.

The third obstacle is attachment, *raag*. When someone views a person or beloved object as the only possible source for their love, then a dependency develops. This person must possess his lover to feel happy and fulfilled. Whenever there is attachment or a dependent relationship then the fourth obstacle called *dwash,* or aversion—which is opposite to *raag,* or attachment—will eventually take place. This is the answer to why the divorce rate is so high. A person or material object can never truly or completely satisfy the need for love and peace of mind. When you become attached to or dependent on someone, you may demand that they be the provider of all your happiness. Since this is an impossible role to fill, it eventually results in disappointment. This disappointment can lead to blame and aversion. Although one can depend on a partner to help in the journey of life, if this person is expected to satisfy and fulfill all desires, it will not work. An interdependence must develop rather than a dependence. In this way people can work and grow together by helping each other but still maintain their ability to be independent when necessary.

The fifth obstacle is *abhinivaysh*, fear of death. Every healthy living being wants to live forever. Even a minuscule mosquito or ant will always try to escape from death. Yet, every living thing, even the most intelligent of all, human beings, must die. This fear saturates to the very depths of one's existence. When someone is afraid of death or has other distorted fears, there isn't an openness to life. Death of the body is a natural part of life.

All of these obstacles can be neutralized through the practice of meditation. One begins to live life in such a way that even though the physical body and mind go through diverse changing experiences and feelings, the true Self is simultaneously experienced to be unchanging, immortal and blissful. You come to understand that the human system functions in this way so you never are bothered by its functioning or expect that it should function differently. Just as you would expect the eyes to see and the ears to hear, you expect the mind to generate thoughts and for you to become involved with them. But when you meditate with your attention on the true Self, you experience an inner state of peace and happiness that is like a well of bliss springing up from inside your own being. One can now discriminate between what is a changing experience which will never bring lasting joy and what is permanent satisfaction, which only exists in the unchanging. One experiences this joy just through one's own existence. Then one's motivation is the pure joy of living and not the fear of failure or loss.

The Troubles that May Arise Through Meditation Practice

It is important to be aware of some of the problems that may arise in your own practice or in your students' practice. The attrition rate will not be as great if you know that these troubles are normal. Then, whenever they arise, you can use them to further your growth rather than as a way to sabotage your results.

1. **Disease *(vyaadhi):*** Dis-ease in the body, mind or senses. This trouble or obstacle may come while you are practicing meditation. Whenever your body or mind is ill it may be difficult to practice. If you know this may happen, you will practice all the laws of good health, diet, exercise, etc., in order to be able to resume you practices as soon as possible.

2. **Lack of interest *(styaan):*** When one feels no interest in making efforts. Sometimes your interest in practicing will be very keen. At other times you may feel your interest waning. If you are aware that this may happen, you will not be alarmed and you will remember to get new inspiration through reading, meeting with like-minded persons (*satsang*) or attending classes to help inspire yourself and not delay or postpone your practice and the result.

41

3. **Doubt** *(sanshaya):* Weakness in one's own power or uncertainty concerning the result of practice. It is normal and understandable for doubts to arise in your mind in relation to the effectiveness or results of your practice. The philosophy of meditation may sometimes seem contrary to everything you have learned before and have been conditioned to believe. Therefore, know that when doubts arise it is healthy because you can challenge these doubts with your own personal practice. Remember that you are like a scientist in a laboratory. You are studying your own mind and system and observing how it functions. Through your observation and personal experiences your doubts will be removed.

4. **Procrastination** *(pramaad):* Whenever one ignores one's practice, delaying the result. Why do people procrastinate? There may be many reasons. The important thing here is to know that the very nature of the human being is to procrastinate at times. Therefore, when you do, nothing is wrong; just know that you are delaying the result. Once you have had a direct experience of the bliss of the Self in meditation, you will always want to return to it. It is just a matter of time.

5. **Dullness, idleness** *(aalasya):* When weakness prevails in the body due to eating wrong foods, meeting with bad company, or living in a climate which creates heaviness of body or mind, and as a result one loses interest in practice. Therefore, it is important to consider this entire system and take care of your body's needs so you don't lose energy.

6. **Lack of enlightenment** *(avirati):* Whenever the mind loses its power to perceive the reality, when it becomes caught up in hankering for the enjoyment of sense objects and tries to attain permanent satisfaction thereby. The illusion is that permanent satisfaction is to be found through the senses and material things. Until you are established fully in the Self this will continue, as when you are dissatisfied the natural tendency is to look for satisfaction in any way you can. Once you have experienced the satisfied state inside, through meditation practice, you will remember that state and will continue to move towards the goal.

7. **Negative understanding** *(bhraanti darshan):* When one begins to think that meditation is not for him and is causing him trouble. Sometimes you might feel that due to your meditation your life is changing. Old friends and associates might seem different to you or may not attract you anymore because you have changed. You might have a new world view. This is an important step in your development because now you will seek out the good company who will inspire you in your growth. Rather than befriending the people who will keep you stuck in old habit patterns and beliefs that weren't working, you will make new friends.

8. **Non-attainment of the desired result** *(alabdha bhoomikatwa):* When one practices, but due to some unknown reason he is not progressing and so becomes discouraged. Self-realization can become another unfulfilled desire. Instead of thinking of it as something that you desire, you can think of it as what you already are. Then how can you not have attained that which you already are? The proof comes as soon as you pause and watch the space. In that pure space you are.

9. **Slip of the state of mind once attained** *(anavasthitatvaani):* When one attains certain spaces of the mind, yet they vanish sometimes. Through your meditation and research on your self you will experience very blissful and profoundly aware moments, days, months or years. Then for some time that state may elude you and you will feel that you have lost it. It is never lost, as it is you. Once you have experienced the fourth state, you will experience it again if you keep up your practice.

These nine troubles are removed through meditation and the repetition of mantra.

CHAPTER 8

YOGIC TRUTH OR MISCONCEPTION?

The Vedas, the *Bhagavad Gita,* and Patanjali's aphorisms were originally written in the Sanskrit language. These writings were then translated with commentaries by many scholars in several languages. Due to the sometimes inaccurate translations from the original language and the experiential nature of these practices, some of the deeper meanings of these teachings have often been unclear or misunderstood. Following are some of the ideas that have been misunderstood, expressed from a clearer perspective.

The state of yoga or union with the Self is achieved when the thoughts in the mind are controlled.

Thoughts do not need to be controlled. Your mind is a field of thoughts and they appear without your invitation. When you come to know that your thoughts are waves of perception that you as the Self use to perceive the world, then your thoughts are not problems that have to be controlled. They appear from the source or Pure Consciousness, and you can observe them as they return back to that same source. When you follow these thoughts back to the source, or experience the space between your thoughts, you are united with the Self. When ice is heated, it turns to water and then steam, which dissolves back into space. H_2O can appear in different forms, but it is the same substance. In the same way, your thoughts can be seen as energy in the more solid form of words, and then as more subtle perceptions, or waves, which you can observe as they dissolve back into the Pure Consciousness field of your awareness. Just as we know the ocean is all water even though we may perceive waves, spray or foam, we can also know that thoughts are all Pure Consciousness.

Lust, anger, greed, attachment and ego are vices and should be removed.

All of these so-called vices are part of the human condition. If there were no lust, then how would procreation happen? If there were no greed, how would anyone save money? If there were no attachment, how would anyone ever stay married, bring up children or own a home? If ego were removed, how would there be a sense of self-esteem or any need for accomplishment? We can see that all of these have a purpose, so why are they called vices? When you are dependent on external things as your sole source of happiness or fulfillment, then these become vices which are problematic. If one needs to continually fulfill their desires through sensual pleasures and attachment to things, or by gaining name and fame, one will soon get disillusioned and become miserable. The one who is free from these vices can use them effectively when appropriate and not to one's detriment. The ego should be expanded to include the whole, knowing it is not just your individual ego or self that is great, but seeing the greatness of all beings and, ultimately, seeing all made from one consciousness or Self.

You have to eliminate all of your desires.

The very nature of the waking state is that as soon as one gets up from sleep there is desire. Without desire why would you even get out of bed in the morning? So you can't stop your desires. Instead, you have to become the master of your desires. If you want to initiate a desire, then you do it. If you want to change it, then you do it. It is not through fulfilling your desires that you will become free and happy. If you seek inner joy and happiness, you will not be dependent on outside things or the fulfillment of your desires to create happiness. Your mind then becomes free from the result of your desires as you are already fulfilled, happy and maintain a quality of stillness or peace.

Your illness is due to your negative thinking.

Your body and mind are inseparable and the thoughts that you are identified with will affect your health. However, this is not the sole cause of disease. Other factors such as heredity, the environment and your diet also contribute to your physical well-being. Major stress to the body, such as accidents and personal loss, will all have an effect. The most important thing to remember is that if you are ill it is not because you are bad or did something wrong. Even the most highly evolved saints and sages have gotten illnesses and died of heart attacks, cancer and other common causes.

When you know that you are more than only a physical body, that you are also spirit, then you can accept more easily the changes the body may need to go through. Just like a machine, it may need to be serviced or operated on. When you meditate, you are filled with energy and this gives your body the maximum ability to heal itself. The *Bhagavad Gita* says that you, the Self, cannot be cut by weapons, wet by water, dried by wind or burned by fire. The Self is indestructible and you must know this. That You is never sick and diseased; it is always perfect.

You have to surrender to God, Guru, or a higher power.

When one thinks of surrender, the common understanding might be that you give up something to someone. This can be misunderstood to mean that you should trust someone outside of yourself more than yourself. If all is the Self, then who is there to give up to whom? More correctly, this can be understood that you as an ego, body and mind need to be aware that these are only some of the aspects of you, which are limited and not omniscient. You therefore give up or surrender your limited understanding, or ignorance, to a higher power or aspect of your own Self, and allow your life to manifest from that perspective.

With this clearer understanding of these spiritual truths, you can stop condemning parts of yourself or the way you are thinking. Instead, you can begin to live from a higher perspective, and function to your highest potential by living in the world and enjoying all the wonderful things life has to offer, and yet not be a victim of your own conditioning or faulty thinking.

CHAPTER 9

THE STRESS RESPONSE AND MEDITATION

Hans Selye (1956), the pioneer of psychosomatic medicine, defined stress as "the rate of wear and tear within the body. The state manifested by a specific syndrome which consists of all the non-specifically induced charge within a biologic system." Stress is necessary to life, and all living things have an innate stress mechanism. Procreation and self preservation could not occur without this innate stress mechanism. In our modern culture, the amount of stress one is subjected to is excessive, and the innate reaction is neither appropriate nor advantageous when it is triggered in many stressful situations. In fact, according to Pelletier (1977), standard medical textbooks indicate that anywhere from 50% to 80% of all diseases are psychosomatic or stress-related. This innate stress response is also known as the "fight-or-flight" response. When human beings are roused to the fight-or-flight response due to stress, they are innately prone to react as animals would by either fighting or fleeing. Much of the stress that we experience cannot be dealt with by either fighting or running away. Such behavior is not considered acceptable in our society.

When your boss informs you that the project that you worked so hard on was not accepted, it would not be appropriate for you to either start a fist fight or leave your job. However, your body still sends messages through your neuroendocrine system which cause significant changes in your biochemistry (Pelletier, 1977). Your blood pressure, heart rate, rate of breathing, blood flow to the muscles, and metabolism are prepared for conflict or escape. This may explain why in an apparent non-emergency situation, such as sitting in traffic or waiting on a long line, you feel so uneasy and stressed. Your body is unable to discriminate between what is a dangerous situation and what is just an uncomfortable situation. Therefore, it reacts with the same fight-or-flight response and the same physiological symptoms as if you were in a dangerous situation. Therefore, you feel as though you need to escape. It can be very frustrating when you can't, as your body is giving you all the cues to fight or run away. That is why in these situations it is imperative to realize your body's lack of ability in this area, and to reverse this reaction so you can calm yourself and be even more effective in dealing with such circumstances.

Hans Selye (1956), in his initial work with laboratory rats, noted that the rats responded physiologically when subjected to extreme stress. There was substantial enlargement of the cortex of the adrenal glands; shrinkage or atrophy of the thymus, spleen, lymph nodes and other lymphatic structures; an almost total disappearance of eosinophil cells (white blood cells); and bleeding ulcers in the lining of the stomach or duodenum. Selye's stress model places heavy emphasis on the pituitary hormone ACTH, which stimulates the adrenal cortex and initiates the general stress reactivity. He has shown how the entire system functions to maximize the body's ability to resist the stressor, and that prolonged stress will wear out the body and lower resistance. When the body fails to adapt, or to overcome stress, diseases that Selye calls diseases of adaptation, or simply ordinary diseases, will develop. Examples of such stresses are divorce, business difficulties, marital problems and chronic illness. It also stated that some stressors might be developmental, such as going to school, leaving the parental home, getting married, becoming a parent, failing to attain occupational goals and retirement.

When the fight-or-flight response is activated, the sympathetic nervous system or involuntary nervous system becomes activated. It acts by secreting hormones such as adrenaline, epinephrine and noradrenalin which increase blood pressure, heart rate and body metabolism. The Relaxation Response leads to a quieting of the same nervous system. Benson (1975) has shown that hypertensive patients can lower their blood pressure by regularly eliciting this response. Benson, along with Stuart (1993), confirmed these earlier findings by showing that patients with hypertension experienced significant decreases in blood pressure and needed fewer or no medication over a three-year measurement period

Dr. Walter R. Hess (cited in Benson, 1975), the Swiss Nobel Prize-winning physiologist, produced the changes associated with the fight-or-flight response by stimulating the hypothalamus within a cat's brain. He then stimulated another area of the cat's hypothalamus and a response whose physiologic changes were similar to meditation, or the reverse of the fight-or-flight response, was created. He termed this response the trophotropic response and described it as "a protective mechanism against overstress belonging to the trophotropic system and promontory restorative processes." Benson (1975) believes that this response in the cat, described by Hess, is the "Relaxation Response" in man.

Meditation, or the Relaxation Response, therefore, counteracts the effects of the fight-or-flight syndrome. Meditation has been shown by Benson (1975) to decrease oxygen consumption, respiration rate, heart rate and blood pressure in those with high blood pressure. Meditation increases the intensity of alpha, theta, and delta brain waves which are the opposite of the physiological changes that occur during the stress response. Benson also discovered that along with the oxygen consumption and alpha wave production, there was a decrease in blood lactate during meditation. Lactate is a substance that is produced by the metabolism of skeletal muscles that is associated with anxiety.

Dr. Pitts, Jr. (1969), of the Washington University School of Medicine in St. Louis, studied a group of patients who suffered from neurosis and frequent attacks of anxiety. He injected into his subjects a solution of lactate or a non-active salt solution. He found that when lactate was injected almost all the subjects experienced an anxiety attack. When the salt solution was injected, the anxiety attacks were not increased. He also injected normal people with lactate, finding that 20% of them experienced anxiety attacks, while none of them did with the salt solution. Therefore, the findings of low levels of lactate in meditators is consistent with the experience which reports a more relaxed, less anxious feeling.

CHAPTER 10

THE RELAXATION RESPONSE

Herbert Benson, M.D., the best-selling author of the book, *The Relaxation Response*, is an associate professor of medicine at Harvard Medical School and the Deaconess Hospital. He is also the president and founder of the Mind/Body Medical Institute. His program consists of a type of meditation practice he calls the Relaxation Response, as well as nutritional counseling, exercise and stress management. It is being utilized at the Mind/Body Medical Institute and many affiliated hospitals throughout the country. The complete program is described in a book by Benson and his colleague, Eileen M. Stuart, RN, C, MS, and other members of the Mind/Body Medical Institute, entitled, *The Wellness Book*. Benson has been engaged in researching meditation practice for almost thirty years in the U.S. and has studied Tibetan monks in India during deep meditative practices.

The basic premise of his teachings is derived from his findings that the Relaxation Response creates physiological changes which are opposite to the stress, or fight-or-flight response. The following chart is adapted from the book *Timeless Healing*, by Herbert Benson (1996), which describes these changes. (See Table 1.) He has also shown that when one elicits the Relaxation Response, the reduction of one's consumption of oxygen that is brought about is even faster than one would experience in sleep. When you go to sleep, your oxygen consumption very gradually decreases until four or five hours later; then it levels out at an average of 8 percent less than the rate you experience when you're awake and at rest. With the Relaxation Response, the rate decreases by 10-17 percent within the first three minutes. Just think of the profound rest the body can receive when you do not have to breathe as hard to sustain your life. All the systems of the body receive a profound rest; all the cells can be rejuvenated and begin to heal and the immune system can also be strengthened through this process.

Table 1

COMPARISON OF THE PHYSIOLOGICAL CHANGES OF THE FIGHT-OR-FLIGHT RESPONSE AND THE RELAXATION RESPONSE

Physiological State	Fight-or-Flight Response	Relaxation Response
Metabolism	Increases	Decreases
Blood Pressure	Increases	Decreases
Heart Rate	Increases	Decreases
Rate of Breathing	Increases	Decreases
Blood Flowing to the Muscles of the Arms and Legs	Increases	Stable
Muscle Tension	Increases	Decreases
Slow Brain Waves	Decrease	Increase

(Table 1 adapted from Timeless Healing, Herbert Benson, M.D.)

The Relaxation Response can be evoked by various types of relaxation and athletic techniques, according to Benson (1996). These include: meditation, prayer, autogenic training, progressive muscle relaxation, jogging, swimming, Lamaze breathing exercises, yoga, tai chi chuan, chi gong and even knitting and crocheting. He states that it only requires two basic steps to elicit the Relaxation Response. The first step is to repeatedly say one word, phrase, sound or prayer to yourself. Engaging in a repetitive muscular activity may also have similar results. The second step is to notice when common, everyday thoughts come and intrude on your focus, then to passively disregard them and return to your repetition. He says that if you are a religious person you can choose a prayer; if not, you can choose a secular focus. He recommends the following words or prayers that can be used:

Secular focus: One, Ocean, Love, Peace, Calm or Relax

Christian: "Our father who art in heaven" or "The Lord is my shepherd"

Catholic: "Hail Mary, full of grace" or "Lord Jesus Christ, have mercy on me"

Jewish: "Sh'ma Yisroel" "Shalom" "Echod" or "The Lord is my shepherd"

Islamic: "Insha'allah"

Hindu: "Om"

For the athletic types of moving meditation, such as jogging, walking or swimming, he recommends paying attention to the cadence of your feet on the pavement or movement in the water - "left, right, left, right" - and then returning to your point of focus whenever thoughts come into your mind. Benson (1996) claims that they have found that runners using this approach will achieve in the first mile the "runner's high" that usually occurs in the third or fourth mile.

As with most types of meditation, it is recommended that you do not concern yourself with how well it is working. If you do not worry about the results, but instead "just let it happen," you will get more benefit. When you worry, you will bring about the stress response, which is the reverse of the Relaxation Response. Benson (1996) also advises that meditation is not about having profound mystical experiences, but is for the purpose of achieving a sense of calm and peacefulness in your daily life. He suggests that the technique can be done for ten to twenty minutes, twice a day. However, he also recommends what he calls "minis," which are bite-size versions of the Relaxation Response, or simply breathing deeply, releasing physical tension and saying your word or sound, etc., to yourself. This can be done any time during the day when you feel stress getting the better of you.

Benson (1996) has coined another phrase called "remembered wellness," which is based on his research on the more well-known term, the "placebo effect." He feels that the scientific community may tend to refer to things "just being the placebo effect" in the same way they may dismiss certain ailments as "just being in your head." He feels that a person's belief in the treatment contributes to a better outcome, so much so that he believes that in some conditions affirmative belief is all that is needed to heal us. Benson (1996) found that in the patient cases that he reviewed, the effect that he calls remembered wellness was 70-80 percent effective, doubling and tripling the success rate that had always been attributed to the placebo effect. He states, "In my thirty years of practicing medicine, I've found no healing force more impressive or more universally accessible than the power of the individual to care for and cure him or herself." According to Benson (1996), remembered wellness has three components:

1. Belief and expectancy on the part of the patient
2. Belief and expectancy on the part of the caregiver
3. Belief and expectancy generated by the relationship between the patient and the caregiver.

The belief or expectation of a good outcome can have favorable restorative power if the favorable outcome belief is from the doctor, caregiver, patient or both. Benson believes that the ideal model for medicine is that of the three-legged stool. One leg is what patients can do for themselves, the second is surgery and procedures, and the third is pharmaceuticals. As we have seen the power of positive beliefs in healing, you can only imagine the harm of its opposite, negative beliefs. This syndrome has been termed and cited in Benson (1996) as the "nocebo effect" (the negative counterpart to the placebo effect, or remembered wellness). Just by being jolted into believing in a life-threatening danger, the body can release excessive amounts of hormones such as norepinephrine, also called noradrenaline. A massive overdose of norepinephrine triggers a chain reaction of biochemical events that can even cause death.

Benson (1996) states, "This is a cycle we must break. When we marinate our minds in negativity and fear, we spur both the nocebo effect and the fight-or-flight response, which have detrimental effects on our bodies and cause us more worry." He suggests the importance of cognitive therapy to identify and counteract negative automatic reactions. These techniques are more comprehensively described in *The Wellness Book* by Benson & Stewart (1993). These methods require that one become more aware of one's distorted cognitions or thoughts, such as, "I am a failure," or "No one likes me," and dispute their validity, thereby restructuring them with more accurate and supportive statements, such as, "I am successful in many things and whenever I feel I am unsuccessful it is a chance to succeed next time" or "I am liked by many people but it is unreasonable to believe that all people will always like me."

Positive affirmations and visualization are techniques that Benson also recommends. He shows how athletes, using visualization in their training by eliciting the Relaxation Response and visualizing their ideal performance, greatly improve their success rate. The theory behind affirmations always brings to my mind the many jingles from TV commercials and songs from my youth that often return to my awareness. Imagine if these commercials or songs all had positive messages, such as you are wonderful, peaceful and loving, instead of you need this product to feel better or you are sad and lonely from the loss of a love. Imagine how much more our internal dialogue would be filled with supportive and life-sustaining suggestions, rather than the sense of lack or loss perpetuated by advertisements and some of the popular country and western or folk songs.

Transformation Meditation is meant to be practiced by people of all religions and faiths. Although yogic meditation may be considered spiritual in nature, it is also a very scientific technique. The beauty of the system of yoga is that it allows for all religious beliefs, as the vision of Oneness incorporates all religious systems by stating that, in essence, they are all one. There are many paths that can lead to the same goal. I feel it is important to understand, however, the power of religious belief for one's health and healing. Yogis have known for centuries that what they term *satsang*, or company of truth, is most beneficial in promoting well-being and the realization of one's true nature or Self. This *satsang* atmosphere can be open to people of all religious beliefs and also to those with scientific viewpoints. In line with Benson's (1996) findings of the importance of fellowship and social support is the often quoted study conducted by David Spiegel, at Stanford University, cited in Benson (1996). Upon assessment after ten years of treatment, women with breast cancer who participated in support groups lived eighteen months longer on average than women who did not. This study also confirms what the yogis have known: *satsang* allows people the opportunity to unite together in an atmosphere of love and support where they can express their feelings, meditate and discuss the knowledge of the Self. This type of forum keeps the participants' attention established in peace and ease unlike other types of meetings where there is debate and conflict. Meditators often report that meditating in a group, and with the guidance of an instructor, is much deeper than when meditating alone at home.

Praying for others has also shown beneficial effects in improving one's health and the health of others. In one study by R.C. Byrd, cited in Benson (1996), almost 400 patients who had once been hospitalized in a San Francisco coronary care unit were studied for ten months. Half of the patients were assigned someone to pray for them while the other half were not. The patients who were prayed for had significantly fewer episodes of congestive heart failure, fewer cardiac arrests and less pneumonia, and required fewer diuretics and antibiotics. This type of benefit from prayer, although more research in this area needs to be done, may also be a way of showing scientifically the yogic theory of Oneness and our inherent interconnectedness. If remembered wellness is of great benefit to the individual, why would not someone's projected remembered wellness also be beneficial? We all know the power of someone's bad or good vibrations projected towards us. When there is tension in the room, the expression is often, "the tension was so thick we could cut it with a knife." Contrary to this is a situation in which peaceful or loving vibrations are felt, such as in a church or house of worship, or any place where people have been meditating. You may even find that your own home becomes more of a sanctuary of peaceful vibrations when you regularly meditate there.

CHAPTER 11

MINDFULNESS MEDITATION

Mindfulness Meditation is a method adapted from the Buddhist system of Vipasana Meditation. The essence of this system is universal and highly adaptable to all. It has been popularized by Jon Kabat-Zinn, Ph.D., best-selling author, founding director of the Stress Reduction Clinic at the University of Massachusetts Medical Center, and Associate Professor of Medicine in the Division of Preventive and Behavioral Medicine. He is currently a Fellow of the Fetzer Institute and has done many years of research on the application of Mindfulness Meditation for people with chronic pain and stress-related disorders, as well as on the societal applications of meditation.

Mindfulness is essentially about wakefulness. When one is present to each moment as it unfolds, then one is said to be mindful. As we have discussed previously, the nature of the mind is to generate thoughts which are often automatic and sometimes unconscious. This system requires one to remain awake and watchful of these thoughts. As Kabat-Zinn (1994) expresses in his best selling book, *Wherever You Go There You Are,* "When we commit ourselves to paying attention in an open way, without falling prey to our own likes and dislikes, opinions and prejudices, projections and expectations, new possibilities open up and we have a chance to free ourselves from the straightjacket of unconsciousness." He suggests shifting the attention from the mode of doing to the mode of being, and to think of yourself as an eternal witness, free from the confines of time. You just watch the moment as it is, without trying to change it.

Watching one's breath is an important component of this system. This technique is used to help bring the attention into the present moment and is recommend by Kabat-Zinn (1994), who states the following:

> Staying with one full in-breath as it comes in, one full out-breath as it goes out, keeping your mind open and free for just this moment, just this breath. Abandon all ideas of

getting somewhere or having anything happen. Just keep returning to the breath when the mind wanders, stringing moments of mindfulness together breath by breath.

This technique can be utilized any time throughout the day. You may even take short breaks from reading this and practice it, as every moment there is the space and time to become mindful. Then this can become a moving meditation as well as a sitting meditation. It is also recommended for more concentrated awareness that you practice it while sitting for five to thirty minutes once or twice per day. People coming through the clinic were asked to practice for forty-five minutes at a time for an eight-week period. The sincerity of one's practices was always seen to be more important than the amount of time spent; sometimes even five minutes could be as effective as forty-five when done with total awareness. For busy professionals such as medical students or corporate employees, fifteen minutes a day, twice a day, is often recommended.

Kabat-Zinn (1994) discusses the meaning of practice and it is similar to the yogic description of the true meaning of *abhyaas,* also usually translated as practice. It is not the same type of practice as one would do when learning a musical instrument or lifting weights. Those types of practice are repetitive for the purpose of rehearsal or improvement. Mindful practice is just fully committing to each moment as it is. *Abhyaas*, or practice, of Transformation Meditation can be defined as the direct observation or experience of the space or gap between the thoughts or images that is always there. Therefore, the practice is the actual result rather then a rehearsal for a future performance or achievement. Kabat-Zinn also expresses, "Rather than doing practice, it might be better said that the practice is doing you, or that life itself becomes your meditation teacher and your guide."

We can observe the similarity and differences between Mindfulness and Transformation Meditation. Both require the impartial watching and observation of whatever is happening. Transformation Meditation expands this observation of what is happening into becoming aware of the very observer who is watching, and also of the space behind or at the back of the thoughts. Without the suggestion of noticing the observer, one might just notice the thoughts and images since most people are trained to see only forms. In Transformation Meditation one expands the capacity of the intellect by bringing the attention to the formless, which is the very source of all form. This may also happen in Mindfulness Meditation, but with this added awareness the observation more rapidly moves to the source or Pure Consciousness rather than only focusing on the form. As we know through science, all forms are the whirling of energy at slower speeds which makes them appear solid. However, they are truly made of energy or Pure Consciousness. Therefore, the practice is in seeing the reality and not just the manifestation of thoughts or images that appear to be real but are in essence energy or consciousness.

Kabat-Zinn (1994) also discusses non-doing as letting things be the way they are, allowing them to unfold in their own way. This is a similar concept to the term from the *Bhagavad Gita, nishkaam karm yog,* or not being attached to the results of one's actions. One engages in action but with the awareness that the very power that allows one to move is the life force. That very life force is always guiding you. It continually guides your breathing and heartbeat and even wakes you up in the morning, without your personal effort. One may also be aware of this guidance of the life force while singing and dancing, or through creative expression in art and writing. In sports, when one has achieved a higher state, it is often referred to as the "zone." At these times, one may have the sense that one is not the doer; rather, the creativity or unlimited energy is just flowing through you. The words of your poem or song may just pop into your head. The pen just appears to move and the story is written, or you are running much further or faster than your mind has believed possible. These are examples that most people have experienced at one time or another, and through this direct experience we can see that by non-doing, one actually is more creative, efficient and successful.

Meditation allows one to tune into this "zone." This state can also be called the field of non-doership, as one remains aware but allows the meditation to unfold however it does. This transposes to other activities in one's life whereby one can also allow life to unfold perfectly without struggle. A rose seed is planted in the soil, and it grows into a bush and then the buds appear. The rose flower petals unfold in their perfect time when given the right amount of sunlight and water. In the same way, our being, when nurtured and allowed to become absorbed in our very sense of being-ness, unfolds the perfect garden of delight.

When one observes the mind without getting caught up with the thoughts, one becomes aware of all the opinions and judgments. Mindfulness Meditation means becoming an impartial observer and not condemning yourself or your thoughts, even the ones that are judgmental. Kabat-Zinn (1994) expresses that our thoughts "usually are merely uninformed private opinions, reactions and prejudices based on limited knowledge and influenced primarily by our past conditioning. When not recognized as such and named, our thinking can prevent us from seeing clearly in the present moment. Just being familiar with this deeply entrenched pattern and watching it as it happens can lead to non-judgmental receptivity and acceptance."

A study conducted by Kabat-Zinn, et al. (1992), was designed to determine the effectiveness of a group stress reduction program based on Mindfulness Meditation for patients with anxiety disorders. The twenty-two study participants were screened with a structured clinical interview and found to meet the DSM-III-R (diagnostic manual used by mental health professionals) criteria for generalized anxiety disorder or panic disorder with or without agoraphobia. Assessments, including self-ratings and therapists' ratings, were obtained weekly before and during the meditation-based stress reduction and relaxation program, and monthly during the three-month follow-up period. It was found that a group Mindfulness Meditation training program can effectively reduce symptoms of anxiety and panic and can help maintain these reductions in patients with generalized anxiety disorder, panic disorder, or panic disorder with agoraphobia.

Carmody, et.al. (2011) conducted a study using Mindfulness-Based Stress Reduction (MBSR), an 8-week group-based training program in mindfulness and its application, to test the effects on hot flash frequency and intensity, including menopause-related quality of life. It was found that many women had used hormone therapy (HT) to relieve their menopausal symptoms, but the risks to health was a cause for concern. MBSR was investigating an effective, safe answer for symptomatic relief for women. The MBSR program displayed itself as an effective adjunctive intervention in reducing medical symptoms and psychological distress. Researchers anticipate that results from this pilot study will provide the data needed for further investigation on the effect of MBSR on hot flash frequency and intensity and the ability to cope with menopausal symptoms.

Mindfulness Meditation has become a valuable system that is widely accepted as a clinical treatment used by mental health professionals, as well as a teaching modality used by teachers and other helping professions. It is being used in many school programs as a method of stress reduction and improved focusing for students, as well as stress management for the teachers themselves. To utilize Mindfulness Meditation in your daily life, for teaching others, or for a mental health treatment modality these proven methods have shown to be effective in the treatment of stress related disorders as well as numerous other mental health diagnoses. For more detailed methods, exercises, tools, as well as skill building, handouts and worksheets for yourself or your clients to assist them in utilizing Mindfulness methods for mood disorders such as: depression, anxiety, panic attacks, post traumatic stress disorder, obsessive compulsive disorder, bipolar disorders, ADHD, anger, as well as other chronic mental illnesses, please refer to Burdick (2013), *Mindfulness Skills Workbook for Clinicians and Clients, 111 Tools, Techniques, Activities and Worksheets*. For more information on teaching and using Mindfulness Meditation with children and teens, you can refer to Burdick (2014) Mindfulness *Skills for Kids & Teens: A Workbook for Clinicians & Clients with 154 Tools, Techniques, Activities & Worksheets*. For an additional continuing education course (soon to be available) using these methods of Mindfulness Meditation, please check our website www.transformationmeditation.com.

Treatment of Chronic Pain and Insomnia

According to a panel at the National Institutes of Health Technology Assessment Conference (1995), chronic pain and insomnia can be helped by relaxation and behavioral therapies. "Relaxation techniques can help slow heart rate, lower blood pressure, and relax large muscle groups - all of which can diminish perception of pain," says Julius Richmond, M.D., professor at Harvard's Department of Social Medicine. He recommends meditation, hypnosis, biofeedback and cognitive-behavorial therapy for chronic pain and insomnia.

In November 1997, Herbert Benson, M.D., addressed the United States House of Representatives Committee on Appropriations and Subcommittee on Labor, Health, and Human Services and Education regarding "Healing and the Mind." Benson states that the treatment of chronic pain becomes extremely costly and frustrating for patients and health care providers. In one study, he assessed clinic usage at an HMO among chronic pain patients who participated in his out-patient behavioral medicine program, of which the Relaxation Response is an integral part. There was a thirty-six percent reduction in clinic visits for over two years in the patients who participated in the behavioral medicine program as compared to their clinic usage prior to the intervention. In 109 patients, the decreased visits projected to an estimated net savings of $12,000 for the first year following treatment and $24,000 for the second year. These savings did not include those realized by the decreased use of medications.

Benson also stated another example of how mind/body interventions can result in better medical care and reduce medical costs in the treatment of insomnia. Approximately thirty-five percent of the adult population experiences insomnia. Half of these insomniacs consider it a serious problem. Billions of dollars are spent each year on sleeping medications, making insomnia an extremely expensive condition. The direct costs to the nation are approximately $15.4 billion yearly and actual costs are astronomical in terms of reduced quality of life, lowered productivity and increased morbidity.

Benson also said that he studied the efficacy of a multi-factor behavioral intervention for insomnia that included Relaxation Response training. Compared to controls, those subjects who received behavioral and relaxation response treatment showed significantly more improvement in sleep patterns. On the average, before treatment it took patients 78 minutes to fall asleep. After treatment, it took 19 minutes. Patients who received behavioral and relaxation response treatment became indistinguishable from normal sleepers. In fact, the seventy-five percent reduction in sleep-onset latency observed in the treated group is the highest ever reported in the literature.

Meditation produces powerful pain-relieving effects in the brain, according to Zeidan, Ph.D. (2011). This was the first study that showed that only a little over an hour of meditation training can dramatically reduce both the experience of pain and pain-related brain activation. This study found about a 40 percent reduction in pain intensity and a 57 percent reduction in pain unpleasantness. Meditation produced a greater reduction in pain than even morphine or other pain-relieving drugs, which typically reduce pain ratings by about 25 percent. For the study, 15 healthy volunteers who had never meditated attended four, 20-minute classes to learn a meditation technique known as focused attention. Focused attention is a form of Mindfulness Meditation where people are taught to attend the breath and let go of distracting thoughts and emotions.

More recent studies were done by Steiner (2014), a pediatric resident at the New York University Langone Medical Center and Bellevue Hospital. He discusses treating chronic pain with meditation. Pain is costly and difficult to manage. A survey on (U.S.) medical expenditure conducted in 2008 revealed that about 100 million adults were affected by pain. *The Journal of Pain,* estimated the cost of persistent pain to be from $560 to $635 billion annually. This far exceeds diagnoses of cardiovascular disease, injury, and cancer. The main treatment for pain is narcotics and opiates—a class of drugs that affects the brain—and have created an epidemic of prescription drug abuse. It is also noted that pain medications ignore the psychological and social aspects of pain. The relentless nature of chronic pain suggests that stress, environment, and emotional effects can intensify the tenacity of the pain. Scientists and researchers have examined the effects of meditation on areas such as: attention regulation, body awareness, depression, post-traumatic stress disorder, addiction, and treatment for pain. Studies discovered that meditation helped reduce pain by activating and reinforcing areas of the brain used in processing pain. Thus, meditation treats pain on every level. It diminishes anxiety surrounding pain and its associated behaviors leaving the patient happier and more in control. Simply put, meditation reduces pain by reducing stress.

Wells (2014), Professor of Neurology at Wake Forest Baptist Medical Center and researchers from Harvard Medical School, found MBSR could significantly help adults who suffer from migraines. In Wells' study it was shown that a group of ten adults who participated in MBSR therapy had less frequent occurrence of migraines of less severity, shorter duration, were less debilitated by them and had a greater sense of control over their migraines than the 9 adults who received standard medical treatment. Based on their study, the researchers also concluded that this technique of meditation was safe and practicable and Wells planned to conduct further studies of larger scale to further evaluate its effect.

Reduction of Stress and Improvements in Overall Health

The cell biologist and psychologist, Joan Borysenko (1987), started the Mind/Body Clinic in Boston's Beth Israel Hospital. This clinic was designed to train patients in the relaxation response. A study by the Harvard Community Health Plan (an organization affiliated with Harvard Medical School) revealed that after going to the clinic, patients reduced their regular doctors visits by half.

Transcendental Meditation (TM), originated by the Maharishi Mahesh Yogi in the sixties, has been a widely researched form of meditation over the past forty years. A study by Orme, Johnson and Schneider (1987) showed that TM reduces the incidence of disease.

The health insurance statistics kept on two thousand meditators over a five-year period showed half the doctors visits and hospitalizations and fewer medical treatments in 17 disease categories for meditators.

In another Orme Johnson (1987) study, TM meditators showed improvement in the factors related to longevity, such as: cardiovascular health, positive health habits, physical function, intelligence and work satisfaction. In more recent studies on TM, MacLean, et. al. (1997), discuss how stress has been implicated in both somatic and mental disorders. The mechanisms by which stress leads to poor health are largely unknown. However, studies in animals suggest that chronic stress causes high basal cortisol and low cortisol response to acute stressors and that such changes may contribute to disease. Previous studies of the TM technique as a possible means of countering effects of stress have reported altered levels of several hormones, both during the practice and, longitudinally, after regular practice of this technique. These results appear to support previous data suggesting that repeated practice of the TM technique reverses effects of chronic stress significant for health.

Mindfulness practice leads to increases in regional brain gray matter density according to Holze, Carmody, et. al. (2011). Participating in an 8-week Mindfulness Meditation program made measurable changes in brain regions associated with memory, sense of self, empathy and stress. A research team led by Massachusetts General Hospital documented that meditation produced changes over time in the brain's grey matter. Their study demonstrated that changes in brain structure may underlie some of these reported improvements and that people are not just feeling better because they are spending time relaxing.

One of the largest public health studies on meditation was conducted by David Sibbritt, et al., (April 2011). This study was based on a representative national survey of 19,209 Australian women. The survey indicates that nearly 35 percent of women in the age group 28 to 33 practiced meditation or yoga. In the 56-61 age range, that figure was 27%. This study focused on understanding the role of meditation and yoga in general well being as well as specific physical and emotional health parameters.

The following conclusions where drawn from the study:

1. General health of regular meditators was significantly better than women who use meditation rarely or never.

2. Meditating regularly resulted in highly significant improvement in mental health. In addition, regular meditators also reported significantly higher level of vitality.

3. In regard to emotional adjustment, the effect of meditation was less significant In the younger group in the study. However meditation was not found to make any positive difference in the quality of life of those who undertook meditation for physical functioning, or bodily pain.

But in the older age group, physical functioning improved significantly in those undertaking regular medication or yoga. But again, meditation had no impact on bodily pain in those who undertook it for that specific purpose.

"As holistic preventive health care is largely absent from modern health care systems, a return to our spiritual roots in the form of meditative practice perhaps signifies that Western medical healthcare has for too long ignored the holistic interaction between the mind and body." (Sibbritt, 2011)

Meditation, according to Pennsylvania neuroscientist Amishi Jha and Michael Baime (2007) director of Penn's Stress Management Program, is an active and effortful process that literally changes the way the brain works. Their study is the first to examine how meditation may modify the three subcomponents of attention, including the ability to prioritize and manage tasks and goals, the ability to voluntarily focus on specific information and the ability to stay alert to the environment. In the Penn study, subjects were split into two categories. Those new to meditation, or "mindfulness training," took part in an eight-week course that included up to 30 minutes of daily meditation. The second group was more experienced with meditation and attended an intensive full-time, one-month retreat.

Researchers found that, even for those new to the practice, meditation enhanced performance and the ability to focus attention. Performance-based measures of cognitive function demonstrated improvements in a matter of weeks. This research was supported by the National Institutes of Health and the Penn Stress Management Program.

Treatment of Heart Disease

The landmark results of Dr. Dean Ornish's research, presented at the American Heart Association's annual meeting in 1990, and published in a leading medical journal and described in his book *Dr. Dean Ornish's Program for Reversing Heart Disease*, have shown the benefits of stress management for cardiac patients. Ornish (1990) studied forty-eight men and women who had coronary artery blockages of 40 to 100 percent. Half of these patients were assigned to a control group that followed the standard AMA recommendations, including exercise, decreased consumption of fats and no smoking. His study group, the other half, followed a strict vegetarian diet and at least one hour per day of yoga, meditation and breathing techniques. Whereas half of the patients in the control group showed an increase in chest pain and arterial blockage, a significant number in the study group showed reduction in artery blockage. In the study group, those who were sickest at the start showed the most improvement. Follow-up studies suggest that the stress-reduction element may be the most significant factor in achieving these results. Ornish believes that yoga, meditation and the group support were essential in obtaining these results and in the continual healing process. His program is now being conducted at hospitals throughout the world.

Duke University Medical Center psychologist, Blumenthal (2002) showed that teaching stress management to heart patients not only helps prevent repeat heart attacks, but also saves money. The benefits of stress management as follow-up care appear to exceed either exercise programs or the usual heart care. The patients were assessed annually for five years. The average costs for those using stress management totaled $1,228 per patient in the first year, compared with $2,352 per patient who exercised and $4,523 per patient for those who received the usual care. Those average costs rose to $9,251 per person in the fifth year for the stress management patients, compared with $15,688 for the exercise group and $14,997 for those receiving usual care. Patients in both the exercise and usual care groups averaged 1.3 adverse cardiac events: bypass surgery, angioplasty, heart attack or death by the fifth year. However, the stress management individuals averaged only 0.8 adverse events. The results extend earlier work that showed stress management programs reduce cardiac events in the short term, and now we can demonstrate a long-term benefits.

Robert Schneider (2012) lead researcher and director of the Institute for Natural Medicine and Prevention in Fairfield, Iowa, hypothesized that reducing stress through the practice of meditation would help lower the risk of cardiovascular disease. A study was performed involving a group of adult African-Americans with heart disease. African-Americans were selected for this study because in the U.S. they have a greater death rate from cardiovascular disease. Participants were divided into two groups; one group practiced Transcendental Meditation regularly, while the other group attended health education classes about lifestyle modification, diet, and exercise, for more than five years. The group that practiced Transcendental Meditation was less likely to have a heart attack, stroke, or die, as compared to the group that attended the health education classes. Schneider concluded that physicians could safely prescribe Transcendental Meditation practice for their patients as a technique for lowering stress and risk of cardiovascular disease.

Cancer Treatment

In an article by Leslie Berger (1999) in the *New York Times*, titled, "A Therapy Gains Ground in Hospitals: Meditation," it is reported that in November 1999, Memorial Sloan-Kettering Cancer Center in Manhattan added new Integrative Medicine Services. These services make use of alternative therapies and are teaching Mindfulness Meditation to reduce stress, pain and anxiety in cancer patients.

Carlson (2015), a psychosocial researcher and lead investigator at the Tom Baker Cancer Centre, said that not only can

Mindfulness Meditation help one feel better mentally, but now there is evidence that it can also influence key aspects of one's biology. It is, therefore, becoming more evident through research that our mental state affects our physical health. Canadian researchers from the University of Calgary, for their study used a longitudinal randomized controlled design with 3 groups: mindfulness-based cancer recovery (MBCR), supportive-expressive group therapy (SET), and a minimal treatment control group (6-hour stress management seminar (SMS) For the first time the researchers found evidence that breast cancer survivors, who attended support groups that inspired the practice of meditation and yoga known as MBCR as well as those who attended SET, positively affected their recovery in that their cellular activity (telomere length TL) was altered. It was therefore, concluded that psychosocial interventions providing stress reduction and emotional support resulted in trends toward TL maintenance in distressed breast cancer survivors

Psychiatric Disorders and Depression

Shannanhoff-Khalso (2004) at the research group for mind-body dynamic, Institute for Nonlinear Science, University of California: San Diego, La Jolla, used a vast array of Kundalini yoga meditation techniques specific for treating psychiatric disorders such as obsessive-compulsive disorder (OCD) as well as a wide range of anxiety disorders, as well as managing fear, tranquilizing an angry mind, and one for turning negative thoughts into positive thoughts. In addition a number of disorder-specific meditation techniques are included that are specific for phobias, addictive and substance abuse disorders, major depressive disorders, dyslexia, grief, insomnia and other sleep disorders.

Group-based psychological treatment called Mindfulness Based Cognitive Therapy (MBCT) was as good or better as treatment with anti-depressants like Prozac in preventing a relapse of serious depression, and the non-drug therapy was more effective in enhancing quality of life. Kuyken (2008), at the University of Exeter and the Center for Economics of Mental Health (CEMH) at the Institute of Psychiatry at King's College in London also concluded that MBCT is cost-effective in helping people with a history of depression stay well for the long term. The MBCT exercises were primarily based on Buddhist meditation techniques and helped the study participants learn to focus on the present, rather than dwelling on the past or worrying about future tasks.

In a statement to the media, Professor Willem Kuyken, explained that people treated with anti-depressants are highly vulnerable to relapse when they stop their prescription drug therapy. "MBCT takes a different approach; it teaches people skills for life. What we have shown is that when people work at it, these skills for life help keep people well.

People with severe and recurrent depression could benefit from a new form of therapy that combines ancient forms of meditation with modern cognitive behavior therapy, early-stage research by Oxford University psychologists, Barnhofer (2002). The results of a small-scale randomized trial of the approach, called Mindfulness-Based Cognitive Therapy (MBCT), in depressed patients is published in the journal *Behaviour Research and Therapy*.

The result indicated that the number of patients with major depression reduced in the group that received treatment with MBCT while it remained the same in the other group. The therapy included special classes of meditation learning and advice on how best participants can look after themselves when their feelings threaten to overwhelm them.

Sundquist et. al. (2014) conducted the first randomized study comparing individual Cognitive Behavioral Therapy (CBT) and group mindfulness treatment in individuals suffering from depression and anxiety. The patients were divided into two groups which practiced either exercises related to CBT, or group mindfulness, for a period of eight consecutive weeks. After these eight weeks, it was reported that the depression and anxiety symptoms decreased equally in the patients of both groups. Sundquist concluded that group mindfulness treatment was as effective a treatment method as CBT for treating these disorders.

Age Related Cognitive Disorders

Luders et. al. (2015) based their study on existing research, which suggested that meditation was an affordable and effective remedy for the natural deterioration of the brain due to aging. The study consisted of a group of long-term meditators and a group of control subjects between the ages of twenty-four and seventy-seven. MRI scanning showed less atrophy in the age-related gray matter of the brain in the group of long-term meditators than in controls. The researchers were surprised to find how extensive and significant the effects of meditation were spread throughout the entire brain. Findings supported their original hypothesis that meditation protects the brain and reduces age-related tissue decline because meditation relieves stress which is toxic to neurons in some areas of the brain that are particularly vulnerable to stress.

Wells et. al. (2013) study at Harvard's Medical Center identified brain changes associated with meditation and its resultant stress reduction, as playing an important role in slowing age-related cognitive disorders like Alzheimer's disease and other dementias. The article discussed how meditation improved brain connectivity and inhibited brain atrophy. Using MRI imaging, the group that engaged in Mindfulness Based Stress Reduction (MBSR) improved significantly and experienced less atrophy. It was found that different types of meditation tap different neural networks and brain areas, and so different meditation practices evidence different types of brain benefits. The researchers concluded that meditation and mindfulness training are important for long-term cognitive health and have the power to increase the volume and connectivity between brain areas that lead to mental and physical well-being.

Psychotherapy and the Treatment of Anxiety

Miller, et al. (1995), at the Department of Psychiatry, University of Massachusetts Medical Center, studied twenty subjects in a Mindfulness Meditation-based stress-reduction intervention. They found that the subjects demonstrated significant reductions in anxiety, as shown by the Hamilton and Beck Anxiety and Depression scores, at post intervention and at three-month follow-up. In a three-year follow-up data was obtained, and ongoing compliance with the meditation practice was also demonstrated in the majority of subjects. They concluded that an intensive but time-limited group stress-reduction intervention, based on Mindfulness Meditation, can have long-term beneficial effects in the treatment of people diagnosed with anxiety disorders.

Urbanowski and Miller (1996), at the University of Massachusetts Medical Center Stress Reduction Program, found that by combining Mindfulness Meditation with psychotherapy, one can simultaneously develop ego strength as well as meaningful experiences of egolessness, even for trauma survivors. The combination of treatments may decrease mental health care utilization, yet enhance the psychotherapeutic process in the era of managed care and cost containment.

A study cited in the Berger (1999) *New York Times* article, conducted by Dr. Sara Lazar and a team of Harvard researchers, studied five people who had been meditating for five years on a daily basis. They were placed inside a magnetic resonance imaging scanner (MRI). They were observed over a 42-minute period where they were asked to stare at a dot on a screen, randomly to generate a mental list of animals and to meditate. A study of the pictures taken of their brain showed that the regions that process emotions and influence cardiorespiratory function were most active during meditation. This verifies what meditators have been claiming all along: they feel calmer and experience quantifiable changes in the body.

Stutkin (2003) of Boston University's Center for Anxiety Related Disorder, found slow diaphragmatic breathing proved just as effective in reducing anxiety as antidepressant drug imipramine.

The Progress of Meditation Training

Dr. Herbert Benson first documented the physiological benefits of meditation nearly forty years ago, and since that time he reports that his findings have been repeatedly confirmed. As cited in Berger (1999), Benson, the cardiologist who coined the term "Relaxation

Response" and founded the Mind/Body Medical Institute at the Beth Israel Deaconess Medical Center in Boston, said, "We cannot keep up with the demand of health professions to learn this." According to Berger (1999), last year Congress gave the National Institutes of Health $10 million a year for five years to expand a network of mind-body research centers and provide training for health care workers in a variety of meditative approaches. In 1997, a panel convened by the Office of Alternative Medicine at the National Institutes of Health recommended all medical and nursing students be exposed to alternative theories and techniques. Meditation practice is included as one of these techniques.

Professor Mark Williams (2008), who along with his colleagues in the Department of Psychiatry at the University of Oxford, that developed the treatment called Mindfulness-Based Cognitive Therapy (MBCT), said, "We are on the brink of discovering really important things about how people can learn to stay well after depression. Our aim is to help people to find long-term freedom from the daily battle with their moods," William said. "One way that the treatment benefits people is helping them to live more in the moment, rather than be caught up in upsetting memories from the past or worries about the future."

In the US in the year 2015 meditation is one of the top ten complementary therapies being used. Ten million Americans now say that they meditate. Many doctors who have read the statistics on the benefits of meditation prescribe meditation for their patients. Many of their patients have reported that they have more energy, higher productivity, and improved health. Meditation is now widely accepted and used in psychotherapy and education. Businesses teaching meditation to their employees have reported lower absenteeism, higher productivity, lower rate of injuries and increase in profits. There have been over 1500 studies since 1930 related to meditation and its effects on the practitioners.

CHAPTER **13**

BRIEF COMPARISON OF VARIOUS MEDITATIVE STYLES

Transcendental Meditation (TM)

This well known form of meditation has been extensively studied and widely used. It is a mantra meditation technique developed by Maharishi Mahesh Yogi. It utilizes a personal Sanskrit mantra that is taught only by a certified teacher. The mantra is to be kept secret and practiced for 20 minutes, twice per day.

Relaxation Response & Respiratory One Method of Meditation

The Relaxation Response is a system developed by Herbert Benson. He recommends the repetition of either a non-sectarian or sectarian word or phrase that can be chosen from a list that he provides. The chosen mantra is then repeated, along with a passive disregard for intrusive thoughts, to elicit a conditioned relaxation response. The Respiratory One Method includes the synchronizing of the mantra with the breath. It is suggested to use this technique for 15 to 20 minutes once or twice per day. Similar techniques also derived from the yogic mantra meditation system are used by Joan Borysenko, Ph.D., and Dean Ornish, M.D.

Mindfulness/Insight Meditation

This technique stems from a form of Vipasana Buddhist meditation. It utilizes watching the breath as a point of focus. The goal is to observe in a detached manner the physical sensations, thoughts and any other phenomena in order to gain awareness and insight. This method requires that in each moment you notice anything that you are aware of without changing it. You then allow it to register with the full awareness as it is, without the distortions created by the filter of the ego of the observer. It is sometimes recommended that one practice for 40 minutes per day, but any amount of time spent in mindful observation is considered to be useful and effective. This technique is used by Jon Kabat-Zinn, M.D.

Mindfulness Based Stress Reduction (MBSR)

Dr. Jon Kabat-Zinn developed the Mindfulness Based Stress Reduction (MBSR) program at the University of Massachusetts Medical Center. Since its inception, MBSR has become a common form of complementary medicine that is used to treat a variety of health problems. The National Institutes of Health's National Center for Complementary and Alternative Medicine has provided a number of grants in order to support research on the efficacy of the MBSR program in promoting healing

Mindfulness Based Stress Reduction is an 8-week training that includes Mindfulness Meditation and yoga. The MBSR program started in the Stress Reduction Clinic at the University of Massachusetts Medical Center in 1979 and is now offered in over 200 medical centers, hospitals, and clinics around the world, including some of the leading integrative medical centers such as the Scripps Center for Integrative Medicine, the Duke Center for Integrative Medicine, and the Jefferson-Myrna Brind Center for Integrative Medicine. Classes in MBSR are taught by physicians, nurses, social workers and other health professionals. To read more about the Mindfulness Stress Reduction Program see Kabat-Zinn (2013). *Full Catastrophe Living: Using the Wisdom of Your Body and Mind to Face Stress, Pain, and Illness.*

Mindfulness-Based Cognitive Therapy (MBCT)

Mindfulness-Based Cognitive Therapy (MBCT) is psychological therapy that is designed to aid in preventing the relapse of depression, specifically in individuals with Major Depressive Disorder (MDD). It utilizes traditional Cognitive Behavioral Therapy (CBT) methods and adds in newer psychological strategies, like mindfulness and Mindfulness Meditation. Cognitive methods could include educating the participant about depression. Mindfulness and Mindfulness Meditation, focus on becoming aware of all incoming thoughts and feelings and accepting them, but not attaching or reacting to them. This mindfulness practice allows the participant to notice when automatic processes are occurring and to alter their reaction to be more of a reflection. Research supports the effects of MBCT in people who have been depressed three or more times and demonstrates reduced relapse rates by 50%.

Transformation Meditation is similar to MBCT. The practitioner is trained to watch all their thoughts like passing waves of perception and to de-identify with them. The de-identification process along with the instruction of concluding positively is similar to cognitive therapy techniques. However, with Transformation Meditation one has the added benefit of becoming aware of themselves as the Knower, forever free from all the thoughts and experiences being observed. This not only allows the meditator to be free from their emotional reactions and to live a healthy normal life but these methods also inspire the meditatior to remain in a peaceful state of supreme psychological health and well-being by realizing their own true Self.

Zen Buddhist Meditation

One sits with crossed legs on a cushion or on a meditation bench. Then, by looking downward, one concentrates on following the breath or maintaining one's posture. As the mind wanders, one brings it back to the breath or posture. Also included in this form of meditation is the pondering of a *koan*, a profound ancient riddle teaching the limits of intellectual understanding.

Tibetan Buddhist Meditation

This form of meditation begins with sitting on a special cushion called a *zafu*. Then one focuses the attention on the breath by returning the attention to the flow of breathing whenever possible. Walking meditation, which concentrates on the motion of the body, as well as chanting mantras and visualizations are also utilized.

Christian Contemplative Prayer

Contemplative prayer is very similar in nature to basic mantra meditation. The mantra to be repeated is the name of God, Christ or Jesus. It is utilized to elicit a contemplative, peaceful state which opens one up to prayer.

Jewish Meditation

Jewish meditation, like other styles of meditation, is a deep focusing of the mind. Chanting of ancient Hebrew prayers is used as well as the study of the *Kabbalah* (the mystical texts).

Transformation Meditation

This technique is adapted from the system of yogic meditation and the teachings of Swami Shyam. It is based on observing or focusing on the space of Pure Consciousness or the Knower of all experience. One can utilize the ancient Sanskrit mantra, *Amaram Hum Madhuram Hum,* or the English, I am immortal, I am blissful, or any other mantra that you choose. The breath can also be focused on as an observation point. This system includes all the aspects of the other mantra techniques as well as the observing meditation technique of Mindfulness Meditation, with the added awareness of the pure knowingness or space that exists behind all the thoughts and techniques. It suggests that one always bring the attention to the Knower, who is the very experiencer of all the thoughts and forms.

Transformation Meditation is meant to be utilized by professionals and their students as the most efficacious and complete system of meditation available today. It is easily integrated into everyday life and doesn't require any secret mantra or membership in any organization. It also helps one to understand the purpose, experience and outcome of meditation, physiologically, psychologically and spiritually. Having this more complete knowledge will expedite the meditation process and allow one to have an understanding of what is happening in one's own mind, body and nervous system while practicing meditation. With this system one is also able to utilize the philosophy of meditation in everyday life through self-inquiry, impartial observation and redirecting the mind to become absorbed into the peacefulness of one's being. The result of which will be the direct knowledge and realization of one's own true nature as pure, free, and forever.

CHAPTER 14

COMMUNICATING FROM ONENESS

In order to teach meditation one must feel relaxed and comfortable while speaking to others. Genetic theory tells us that we are all 99.9% alike in our gene structure. It is just that small percentage of differential DNA that makes us into individuals. Many religions tell us that we are created from the same source or in the likeness of God. Therefore, we are really more alike than different. Yogic theory tell us that our essential nature or Self is one Self or consciousness operating in different body forms. The following quote, from an unpublished talk of my meditation teacher, Swami Shyam, gives the essence of how to express oneself when communicating from the vision of Oneness:

> Communication is never between two separate beings; the Self is always interacting with various forms of its own Self. Those who are firmly established in this knowledge always feel easy while interacting because they know the Self alone is both the speaker and the listener. Thus, their language and expression have the capacity to connect all forms of their own Self to the vision of Oneness.

This quote immediately leads our attention away from dualistic thinking, which says we are all individual separate beings, to the vision of Oneness. This higher vision unfolds the perspective that we are all made of the same life-source or consciousness, which we call Self.

Arguably, people's greatest fear is public speaking. It has been said that more people fear this than even death. If one analyzes why this is, we can say that people are afraid of looking unintelligent, not pleasing others, going blank or exposing one of their perceived inadequacies. This shows how rampant the sense of duality is. As we are all human beings with minds and senses and experiences, we can't know everything or be perfect in every situation. When we see other people as others who will judge, criticize or reject us then this fear arises. When we see others as our own Self with the same system that has strengths and weaknesses, certain abilities and certain areas of ignorance, then this problem doesn't arise.

We were once all babies and as babies we were born pure. Babies never fear whom they pee on or whom they cry in front of or how knowledgeable they look. Adults never judge a baby for this lack of ability; they just know babies aren't able to be any different. Personality traits that are not congenital, including some strengths and weaknesses, are developed through life experiences. Our essential nature is pure; however, on the mind and personality level people are only able to do the best they can based on their heredity, learning, upbringing and development into adults.

When someone is in a situation where they are going to speak out loud, whether in a group or with another individual, their nervous system can react with the fight-or-flight response, or stress response. The heart rate increases, palms can sweat and the mouth becomes dry, etc. This is sometimes known as stage fright, or an anxiety or panic attack. This response needs to be understood and reinterpreted. Emotion is just energy in motion. We need energy and enthusiasm to speak and to be effective. You know how bored you can become with a monotonous voice or a speaker who is too laid-back or uninspired. When your energy is balanced through the practice of meditation it can be channeled properly and used to your advantage.

Once the anxiety is balanced and you can speak easily and clearly, the next challenge is to speak in a way that is pleasing to others. Why do people say things that are hurtful? Why do people criticize others or try to prove they are right or to get their egos stroked? This is the nature of the individual human mind. It functions in a way that it appears, falsely of course, that its survival is based on being right and on proving or telling others that they are wrong. The mechanism of human psychology is to attack or defend. Even when you speak in a very normal way, the listener may think you are attacking; and when they defend themselves, you may feel that their defense is an attack on you. This mechanism continues on both sides and in this way you and the other person become two separate parties. The very nature of the mind is that it is formed in each individual by its own life experiences, desires and needs, whether real or imagined. What most people think will bring them happiness, such as material wealth, name and fame, etc., will only bring temporary happiness. Yet the mind is set up to function in a way that it will keep pursuing maximum gain and avoiding loss or pain. Happiness based solely on gain or loss changes; therefore, it is not the true source of happiness.

I am proposing a new way of communicating based on the premise that the purpose of communication is to please one another. Everyone should come to know his or her greatness. As a teacher or communicator it is your purpose to create a nice atmosphere for learning. You can create an environment that allows the vision of Oneness to unfold. When you rely on your own internal source of happiness based on the knowledge that is gained in meditation, you experience your own blissful nature that doesn't change. Then you are not communicating for the sake of ego gain, but for the sake of Oneness. When you communicate with knowledge of your own Self everywhere, you create a sense of joy and the spirit of unity and appreciation all around you. Your life then becomes saturated with these qualities. Try one week of only appreciating everyone and everything. See the magic that will unfold.

A Tale of Two Ants

The following is a cute story that my meditation teacher once told, which demonstrates how people see things from their own perspective.

Two ants met. One had a salt ball in its mouth. The one who did not said, "Come and taste my sweet mountain of sugar." The ant carrying the salt ball replied, "It would be my greatest pleasure to go to your home and taste your mountain." They traveled together and reached the mountain and began to eat. But the salt ball ant couldn't taste the mountain of sugar and said, "Don't tell me lies. Your mountain is as good as my mountain." The first ant said, "It is sweet." But the other ant said, "It is salty." The first ant analyzed the situation and asked, "Why is it that although his body and his tongue are the same as mine, he tastes salt?" Why does one person think one way and someone else think differently?

The sweet ant said, "Come to the waterfall. We should gargle together." When both reached the water and gargled, their mouths were clear and the salt ball dissolved. Then they walked back to the mountain. The first ant said, "Would you like some refreshments? The whole mountain is food." The second ant began to taste that it was all sweet. He said, "You were telling me the mountain was sweet at the wrong place. It was salty over there, but here it is sweet." They walked for awhile, reached where they had started the journey from, and again ate. "Why is it that before I thought it was salty and now it is sweet? Do you have some magic?" The first ant said, "When you came from your home you brought your salty breakfast in your mouth. When you gargled it was washed away." Then the salt ball ant realized that as long as he brought with him a salt ball he would not be able to taste the sweetness of the mountain. In the same way, as long as one is stuck in their own preconceived ideas, beliefs and dualistic type of thinking, then there will always be conflict and one will not be able to taste the sweetness of life, unconditional love and the joy of interacting. Each intellect carries its own salt ball, a sense of difference, which cannot be changed because of the salt ball of duality in the intellect. When freed from these conditions, and resting in the sense of acceptance of all as they are, one will remain open and loving in their communication. Then while teaching meditation, one will accept everyone's perception as it is and still be able to lovingly convey the knowledge of Oneness of the Self.

Answering Students' Questions

There is a definite art to answering the three types of questions that your students may ask. Most questions are straightforward and the student may be searching for a direct answer. Other questions can be more personal and require more skill. The third type of question is a confrontational question which is meant to undermine your authority and/or to confront your ability or the philosophy. These questions will arise due to an individual's sense of duality or internal conflict. They may enjoy participating and their inner being may resonate to what you are saying, but their conditioning and experiences may be contrary to what you are saying.

Therefore, they may feel a need to confront your perspective or to believe that you are wrong.

1. **Direct Questions:** This arises when a student is having difficulty in their meditation and wants some insight into what they are doing. It is always important in this instance to never give them the impression that they are wrong or can do anything wrong. The way I was brought up as a child was to learn through criticism and berating. We don't want to continue that destructive system which makes people weak and insecure, and creates low self-esteem. Instead, we want to start with the premise that everyone is perfect in essence and our very own Self. Therefore, there is nothing wrong or no mistake. You can guide them from wherever they are to the next step of where they need to be. For example, someone asks the question, "How can I get rid of all the thoughts that I have in my meditation?" Or they also may complain about not experiencing the bliss you are talking about, but instead they experience agitation on the level of the body and the mind. In this circumstance it is important to allow them to see that meditation isn't only about getting to the bliss. It is developing the awareness of the observer or Knower. You can bring their attention to who it is who knows they were having these thoughts, or not experiencing the bliss. This will allow them to see that the mind just functions that way, but the one who is watching, the Knower, is where they are training themselves to place their attention.

   Another common question would be about seeing lights or crystals or visions. Some people will see these things and others will not. In your answer it is important that you acknowledge whatever they experience as perfect and at the same time bring the attention back to the Knower. Any experiences they have are on the level of just that, experience. Therefore, you want to bring the attention back to the blue-black space which is free from experience and is permeating even the white light. That can be done by telling them to observe the space in front of their closed eyes and by again placing the attention on the Knower of that experience.

2. **Personal Questions:** This type of question will range from topics of low self-esteem, depression and anxiety, to problems with

their spouse, or family members or friends. In answering these questions you have to know your role here as a meditation teacher. It is not to diagnose or treat psychological conditions. Therefore, your answers, unless you are also trained otherwise, should remain in the realm of meditation and the philosophy of *Yog*. Therefore, you have to remember the basic premise of *Patanjali Yog* which says that the root cause of suffering is ignorance of the Self. The attention should be brought back to the knowledge of the Self, immortal and blissful. The fourth state of consciousness is always free from problems and pain, just as is the deep sleep state. Then guide their meditation so that they can have this experience. Many of the stories that I have told in this manual are good to use as graphic examples of how to be free from the body and mind mechanism where pain is experienced.

3. **Confrontational Questions:** First, it is important for you to be holding the awareness that it is your own Self asking the question. Then that aspect (personality) of your Self doesn't have to agree with your idea. Therefore, anything they say is fine with you. You don't need to get defensive or argue with them. This type of question can create a negative energy in the room. Everyone gets affected by one person's negative space, criticism or blame. Therefore, answering this type of question takes a lot of skill. You must remain free and unaffected by the question. Just know that everyone has a right to their opinion and point of view. Your ability to do this will be based on how effective your own practice of meditation has been and how free you are from the identification with their words or criticism.

Sometimes nothing more than the following type of response is required: "Your perspective and point of view are appreciated." If there is an opening for them to go further (this statement may help to create an opening), then you can gear your talk back to your point. The most important thing for you is to keep the atmosphere and space positive, supportive and free and not to get caught in this person's negativity. The person may say something like, "I think it is good to have powerful emotions and to get angry and condemn someone who is wrong. It sounds to me like you are saying that you should love everyone and I don't think that is healthy." First, I would thank them for their insight and perspective. Then I would initiate the idea that meditation is about mastery and freedom. They have the freedom to feel any way they choose, but it is important for them to decide what type of space they want to live in and to examine how effective this type of thinking and communicating is in bringing them what they truly want. Does it make them feel good temporarily or does it bring a lasting sense of fulfillment, contentment and harmony in their relationships? Let them find the answer themselves rather then telling them how it should be.

Others may question your knowledge or authority. Again, you can support their perspective and tell them this knowledge reaches beyond perspective to our very essence of being. They are free to accept it or not, and to use whatever works for them and reject the rest. That is the beauty of all these techniques: they are experiments that you perform on yourself and you can observe for yourself the benefits; you don't have to believe anyone.

Chapter 15

Teaching Breathing Techniques and Meditation

This chapter will explain the science of breath, *praanaayaam*. You can give your students a copy of this chapter, starting with the next paragraph, along with the handouts in the Handouts Manual that give step-by-step instructions for the techniques. Because sitting still may be difficult for those who have agitated bodies and restless minds, teaching a breathing technique before meditation is extremely useful. It will calm the physiology quickly and enable the person to sit comfortably.

If someone were to ask you if you know how to breathe you probably would laugh. We all know that breathing is necessary for life; however, the way you breath has an effect on your overall health and state of well-being. *Praanaayaam,* or breath control, is an ancient yogic system that increases energy and creates balance and overall health. Certain techniques were developed to regulate one's energies by training the breathing mechanism. The breath is the part of the autonomic nervous system that is both automatic and voluntarily controlled. You can't control your heart rate or blood pressure at will; however, you can easily control your breath. The breath is very closely linked with the emotions. When one is calm, the breath is deep and slow. When one is tense, angry or fearful, the breath is held or becomes irregular, short or difficult. Therefore, by controlling the breath one can regulate the emotions and create a sense of calmness. These techniques have also been known to strengthen the nervous system and to switch on the parasympathetic part of the autonomic nervous system. This can be very helpful for those restless nights when you are trying to fall asleep and your mind keeps racing with all kinds of thoughts. By changing one's orientation from a sympathetic or more active mode to a parasympathetic mode, one's nervous system can rest, relax and repair.

The technique of deep abdominal breathing (described on page 138 of the Handouts Manual) helps to move the diaphragm so that it presses on the lower portion of the lungs and releases all the carbon dioxide as one exhales. There is then room to expand the abdomen on the inhalation and to take in a larger supply of fresh oxygen. This oxygen and *"praan,"* or life force energy, that are taken in with the breath then oxygenate and revitalize all the cells, organs, glands and the brain. When one is anxious the lungs fill with carbon dioxide and the introduction of fresh oxygen is difficult. This often occurs during an anxiety or panic attack. The lungs fill up with carbon dioxide and cannot take in oxygen. You feel as if you cannot breathe. Diaphragmatic breathing then helps you to exhale all the carbon dioxide and makes room to bring in more oxygen. The fresh oxygen creates a calming effect and strengthens the nervous and immune systems. This type of breathing also reverses the stress response by providing more oxygenation of the blood. This results in greater mental acuity and improved general health.

Another technique, called alternate nostril breathing, involves alternately inhaling through one nostril and then exhaling through the other. If you check throughout the day you will notice, unless your nose is stuffed due to a cold or allergy, that one nostril is usually more open than the other. This seems to switch every few hours over the course of the day. In right-handed people, when the right nostril is clogged and the left is more open, then the right side of the brain or the creative side is dominant. Conversely, when the left side is clogged and the right nostril is more open, the left side of the brain, or the analytic side, is more active. If you are having trouble with creativity or being analytical or even sleeping at night, it's interesting to check which nostril is more open. By using the alternate nostril technique, you can balance the right and left sides of the brain, soothe and purify the nervous system, and cleanse and open the nasal passages. This normalizes the metabolic process and combats the detrimental effects of stress.

Longevity can be measured by the number of breaths one takes per minute. Dogs and cats have a faster breathing rate then humans, so their life span is shorter. Those species that breathe at a slower rate per minute live longer. They do not need to take in as much oxygen to sustain the body. The lungs and heart do not have to labor as hard and vital energy is conserved. If you want to live a longer and healthier life, then take up this practice of *praanaayaam*; your great-grandchildren will be glad you did.

Meditation Techniques

Based on the theory and philosophy of meditation you have studied so far in this course, you should have an excellent foundation for knowing how to teach meditation. Also, you will have the direct experience from your own practice. The Handouts Manual has a step-by-step guided meditation, called "This Is Meditation," that can be studied and memorized to assist you in guiding your students in meditation. The course outline in Chapter 16, as well as the guided meditations on both audio recordings, will also assist you in teaching beginning students meditation.

There is an infinite variety of ways to guide a meditation. Most important is that you are in meditation yourself when guiding. Students will get the full experience of your peaceful space which they entrain with, as that peace is also within them. The audio recording, *Infinite Peace*, also has two guided meditations which you can listen to several times to familiarize yourself with the technique of guiding a meditation.

In Transformation Meditation a variety of techniques are used to bring you to know the space that you are meditating on. That space appears as soon as you close your eyes. Therefore, mantra is used so that the meditator can experience the very space that is behind the mantra. However, you might first like to have a few sessions of teaching just the mantra technique before adding this component. After guiding the students in the basic steps to mantra meditation, and once they have repeated the mantra several times to themselves, you can ask them to take a few moments to focus on who it is that is knowing that they are repeating the mantra. That will immediately bring their attention to the space of knowingness which is free from the mental activity. "Four stages of Mantra Meditation," outlined in the Handout Manual, can be used to guide your students in a more advanced meditation. (The following lesson plans will guide you in teaching the full technique.)

Chapter 16

Lesson Plan for Five-Session Series and Beyond

These lesson plans for this series of classes can best be explained on audio recording. Therefore, this chapter is a basic outline of what you will hear in greater detail on the teacher training audio recording. Each lesson topic also has a page in the Handouts Manual.

Foundation Series of Five Classes

Each class can last for an hour and a half.

Class 1

A. **Introduce yourself and the class:** Give a short introduction which includes your qualifications, your background and how you have benefited from your own practice. Get feedback from the class by asking each person to say their name, if they have meditated before and what they hope to gain from the class. If it is a large group, then you can ask for a show of hands indicating whether or not they have meditated before, and you can ask them to answer the following questions: Did they come to this course to reduce stress? to help with anxiety? to help with physical problems such as high blood pressure, a cardiac condition, chronic pain? or to open up spiritually?

B. **Breathing technique:** Discuss what *praan* is and how the breathing techniques work (see Chapter 15). You can guide the class in deep abdominal breathing according to the instructions in the Handout Manual and on the teacher training audio recording. Get feedback from the class as to what they have experienced. Do not imply that they have to become relaxed immediately, as for some students this will be new and will take some time to learn. Other students will relax even by practicing this technique for just two minutes.

C. **What is meditation:** Give them a working definition of meditation. Meditation is a state of higher awareness. (Chapter 1,

Transformation Meditation Is More Than You Think!, will give you the information for this class, as will "This is Meditation" in the Handout Manual and on the teacher training audio recording.) Make sure to tell the class that the biggest misconception about meditation is that one shouldn't think or have thoughts during meditation. Thoughts are natural and are not a problem to the meditator. Thoughts can come and go; it is the space that they come from and go to that we place our attention on. Introduce the information on the four states of consciousness and explain the fourth state or *turiya* state.

D. Benefits according to research: Give an overview of the benefits of meditation. Bring in the points that the students mentioned as to what they hoped to gain from the course. Base this section on what the class is wanting to know. If they want information on physiological or psychological benefits, see Chapters 9-12 and review the sheet, "How Stress Affects You," in the Handout Manual. If they want information on spiritual or other benefits, give them an overview from your readings in Chapters 1-8.

E. Explain the techniques of meditation: Start with a simple technique of watching the breath going in and out or a simple mantra. You can use part of the full mantra, or *aum hum*. Then instruct them to allow the thoughts to come and go and, whenever they remember, to repeat the mantra. It doesn't matter how many thoughts come, or if there are no thoughts. Allow everything to happen and to be part of the meditation. Just like a scientist doing an experiment, you become the observer of your own mind. You are not trying to make anything special happen, you are just watching what happens when you practice this technique. Have them practice for five to ten minutes, depending on how still or fidgety the group is. If still, you can have them sit longer, but you don't want them to sit too long and feel uncomfortable. (Listen to the recording, *Infinite Peace*, for an audio example of how to guide them in this meditation.)

F. Practical aspects: Share with them what times are good for meditation: right after getting up in the morning, before dinner or before bed. It is important to have a regular time at least once per day and preferably twice. It is also good to have the same place or seat in a quiet place if possible, though not essential. They can start with as little as three to five minutes; as they become comfortable with it, the time can be increased. They can sit up comfortably on a chair or on the floor, leaning on the couch or bed for back support. It is only good to meditate in bed if they are trying to fall asleep or right upon awakening, for a few minutes, before starting the day. Otherwise, it is better to find a different place, as the bed is associated with sleep. One should practice meditation when one is alert and able to focus. Meditation is different from a relaxation technique, as one is not only relaxing, although relaxation can be the result of meditation. Meditation goes beyond relaxation as one is transforming one's awareness and developing the ability to live in the fourth state of consciousness. (See Chapter 1.)

Class 2

A. **Review of last class:** You can briefly refresh everyone's memory of what you covered in the last class. This can also be done by asking the students what they remembered. You can ask them to share what they experienced over the week in their practice, and ask for questions. You can then lead them in the breathing techniques they learned last week and a short meditation.

B. **Stress and the fight-or-flight response:** Discuss the information from Chapter 10. As meditation can be the most difficult to practice when you are more agitated or stressed out, you can introduce them to a way of getting settled enough to be able to meditate by following the steps in the process from their manual on *How to Reverse the Stress Response into the Relaxation Response.* This will help them to be able to meditate when it is needed the most.

C. **Introduce mantra:** Define mantra as *man* meaning mind and *tra* meaning to release. There are various systems for how a mantra can be given. Sometimes the students can be asked to choose their own from a list. Sometimes there is one from their spiritual beliefs that they might like to use, such as *amen, sha-lom* or *om*. In the system I use, the mantra *amaram hum mad-huram hum* is passed down from teacher to student. My mantra was given to me by my teacher and therefore it is the mantra I teach in this system of Transformation Meditation. You should feel free to use it and pass it along to anyone you share meditation with. Your students can also then pass it along to anyone with whom they share the practice of meditation. It is in the Sanskrit language which is the original language of the system of yogic meditation. It is a vibrational language and the *aum* or *hum* sound is known as the highest vibratory sound; just by repeating the sounds contained in this mantra one will feel peaceful. You can introduce the meaning of the mantra: *amaram* means immortal; *hum,* I am; and *madhuram* means blissful. I like to explain this meaning so that it doesn't interfere with anyone's spiritual or lack of spiritual beliefs. From a scientific viewpoint, it means that the energy that we are in essence can never be destroyed and therefore is immortal; from a spiritual perspective, it can fit into one's own beliefs regarding the spirit or soul that goes on after death. You can have them repeat it out loud, to make sure the pronunciation is correct, and then silently inside. It can also be very useful to repeat it, or even sing it to a tune out loud together, for up to twenty or so repetitions before continuing to repeat it inside in silence. Repetitions out loud will help to get one used to the sounds and assist in the ability to continue with the silent repetitions. (Listen to the audio recording, *Infinite Peace*, for instructions on teaching this.)

D. Alternate nostril breathing: Teach them this technique which is in the Handout Manual and discuss the benefits. You can end with a short meditation after they complete the technique. (Also listen to the instruction on both audio recordings.)

E. Homework: Encourage them to practice at home. This is a good time to allow them to acknowledge to themselves how they feel now after meditating, and to remind them to make it a daily practice.

Class 3

Each class, after your own short introduction to the class topic, should begin by giving the participants a chance to express. They can let you know if any questions or experiences came up from the prior week's class or from their week of home practice. They may say they are not practicing at home. In that case, you can reassure them that if they keep attending classes and introducing a little meditation at home, even just five minutes per day, then after about six weeks of practice they will develop a new habit pattern. This will make their daily practice much easier. You can then lead a meditation to bring all the group energy together. As the sessions progress and meditation becomes more comfortable, the silent sitting time can become longer, until eventually, by the last class of the series, they are comfortable sitting for at least twenty minutes.

A. **Introduce knower, knowing, known:** Explain to the students the concept of the true Self which is the Knower of the mind, and how this Knower can know the objects or thoughts and feelings, and how, through this process of Knowing, it experiences the world. (Listen to the audio teacher training recording for a more detailed explanation of this process.)

B. **Non-meditator's mind/meditator's mind:** You can use the diagram in the Handout Manual to explain to your students how the Self or Knower begins to identify with the mind and its thoughts and concepts. It shows that depending on whether one's thoughts are positive or negative, one will become happy or unhappy. When one experiences happiness due to this identification process it will ultimately result in inherent unhappiness. This type of happiness is based on the achievement or acquisition of something outside of oneself and, therefore, it will change when the situation changes. The "Meditator's Mind" on the diagram shows how the intellect of the meditator becomes purified and no longer engages in this same identification process; it de-identifies with the mind and the thoughts and experiences one's essential nature which is all peace. (This is explained more completely on the teacher training audio recording.)

C. De-identification process: This experiential exercise, explained in "The De-identification Process; Six Steps to Freedom from Disturbing Thoughts and Feelings" (p. 141 of the Handout Manual), will present the students with the ideas discussed on the chart of the non-meditator's mind/meditator's mind so they can notice how this works within themselves. You can guide them in this process for their final meditation of the class. Afterward you can ask them what they experienced during this process. Be sure to end the class with a brief meditation if a lot of discussion ensues from this question. It is always nice to start and end the class with a unifying meditation, even if just for three minutes. (This process is also described on the teacher training audio recording.)

Class 4

A. Overview of the various meditation techniques

1. Guide a meditation from the Handout Manual using "This Is Meditation."

2. Explain the various techniques (see Handout Manual).

B. Progressive deep relaxation: You can use the sheet in the Handout Manual and either memorize this or read it to your students.

1. Go over what you will be guiding them in and the benefits.

2. Read the deep relaxation technique from the Handout Manual or play it from the recording, *Infinite Peace*.

3. Ask them to again sit up straight facing you and then guide them in a breathing technique and a meditation (see the handout sheet "Various Meditation Techniques" or listen to the recording, *Infinite Peace*).

Class 5

A. Philosophy of meditation: After starting the class with a breathing technique, guide a meditation using the three stages of man-

tra meditation. You can first explain these stages and then see if they can imagine experiencing them. (See the Handout Manual and the teacher training audio recording for the Sanskrit pronunciation.)

B. The state of Yog - union with the Self: Now you can begin to get into the topics on the philosophy of meditation. (See the Handout Manual and listen to the teacher training audio recording.) You can read the handout and explain it in detail from your own understanding after reading all the writings in the Teacher Training Instruction Manual.

Intermediate Series of Five Classes

Classes 1-5

You can start this new series of classes with introductions as you did with the Foundation Series. Then have a short meditation to get everyone's energy more centered in the room to begin each class and end each class.

A. Topics: This five-class series can consist of the following topics, each of which is described thoroughly on sheets in the Handout Manual. For the *Sanskrit* pronunciation please listen to the teacher training audio recording.

1. Three types of pain (see Chapter 3)

2. The eight limbs of yoga, *asthang Yog* (see Chapter 6)

3. The levels of meditation, the *samaadhis* (see Chapter 6)

4. The troubles that have to be removed, the *klayshas* (see Chapter 7)

5. The obstacles (see Chapter 4)

B. Guided Meditation: It is always nice to start and end the class with a meditation. One sitting should be about 20-30 minutes and the other one can be shorter, and even a third one of just two minutes can be added at the end of the class.

C. Breathing techniques: Introduce *kumbhak,* breath retention (see Intermediate breathing techniques in the Handout Manual). You can use the first three techniques, one at each class, and then for the fourth and fifth class you can combine all the techniques. (Listen to the teacher training recording for Sanskrit pronunciation.)

D. How to continue: Since meditation is a life-long process and study, you can organize more classes or ongoing sessions to help them continue their practice. There are other topics in the Teacher Training Instruction Manual that you can use for these classes or find new topics through your continued study. It is nice to have a group that meets at least once per week to keep reinforcing and supporting the students in their practice.

CHAPTER 17

HOW TO PROMOTE YOUR SERVICES

1.   Where to conduct your classes

If you are already affiliated with a hospital, clinic or counseling center, that may be the best place to start. The following is a list of other successful places to teach your classes:

- Schools (continuing or adult education programs)
- Health clubs and spas
- Medical offices, chiropractic and holistic centers
- New age churches
- Yoga centers
- Community centers
- Wellness programs at hospitals
- Pain management clinics
- Rent your own room at a center

2.   Your Brochure/Pre-registration

There is a sample brochure in the Samples Manual for you to utilize in developing your own brochure. You can also develop an e-brochure on your own or using an internet mailing company such as enflyer.com, constantcontact.com, or mynewsletterbuilders.com.

A. What to include in your brochure: Your brochure should tell people what they will learn and what benefits they will receive from taking your course. Of course, it should include the time, place, format, address and phone numbers to call, as well as something about you, the instructor. Comments from former students about your teaching and the benefits they have received are also highly effective.

B. How to register: You should always have a registration form on your brochure or website. This way interested persons can mail or email in their registration, or pay online, effortlessly. There should also be some incentive for them to register in advance. Advance registration is important. When a person has the enthusiasm developed through reading about your program, they are most likely to register. If they wait, they may put it aside and forget about it as the stresses and responsibilities of daily life take over. Therefore, it is a great incentive to suggest an additional free class and/or a reduction in tuition for early registration.

3. The best and the worst methods of advertising

A. The best: Find your target market. It is important that you spend your advertising dollars wisely by focusing on the people who will most likely be interested in your services. Repetitive advertising to the same person is essential. It is said that the person has to see the ad or brochure on an average of at least three times before responding.

- **Your center, clinic or hospital:** They will have a newsletter, mailing and email list. You can also distribute your own brochures there (see copies in the Samples Manual) by putting them out in the office. It is important that you follow up by making sure that you have a write-up in the newsletter and that you speak to other people in the office about your classes so they will refer students to you.

- **Developing your own mailing list:** The best mailing or email list is developed from the people who have shown interest in your programs. Brochures can be emailed by using an e-newsletter company that holds and maintains your email lists. They will assist you in emailing your HTML brochure or newsletter. To acquire your list you can use some of the methods listed below.

- **Yellow pages listing:** If you get a business line, you will receive a listing under Meditation. This is a great source of receiving phone calls from interested, prospective students. People who call you are your best prospects. You don't need a large ad as there will probably not be too many listings in your area.

- **Community calendar announcements:** Most newspapers have listings of classes and programs in the area. You can submit these usually two weeks in advance by email, fax or mail. Some newspapers will list all local classes; others will only list non-profit organizations and/or free classes. In that case you can do a free introductory class or session by appointment when you receive enough responses. This should only be introductory and will give people the opportunity to sign up for your course at that time. To those folks who call you, you can even mail the information about your course, as well as set up a time to meet with them personally for a free session.

- **Small ads and free telephone consultation:** You can place ads in specialty newspapers devoted to new thought. These ads should state that people can call you for a free phone consultation. Many people aren't familiar with what meditation is. This will make them feel comfortable in calling you to receive more information.

- **A website:** if you are teaching meditation independently and do not already have your own website, then, it is important that you either develop your own webpage, have a listing on another website, and/or create social media pages. If you are teaching at a center, hospital, or school, you can ask to post your webpage (that includes your photo, bio, etc.) on their website. Some people decide not to have their own website as it can be time consuming and expensive to develop, host and market. Instead, you can use social media pages such as Linkedin and Twitter, and have a Facebook company page. With this you can also use e-newsletters, sent to your mailing list and posted on your social media pages, these can allow your prospective students to register for your courses by credit card.

If you decide to create a website, you cannot plan that your website alone will bring in new business unless you are willing to spend money to advertise or acquire many links to it through direct email networking, or using social media. It will benefit you to pay to advertise your website if you are teaching many classes regionally, internationally, or online, and if you have books, courses, CDs or other products to sell. Search engines are a good place to advertise as well as online e-newsletters and social media ads that support your region and topics of interest. If you are only teaching locally then your webpage can work like a brochure or business card. People can go to your website to learn more about you and your programs. You can post your class schedule and background information, and also allow them to register for your courses by credit card. It is easy to set up a business PayPal account to receive credit card payments. You only pay them a percentage when someone pays you.

- **Social media:** If you decide not to have a website, or use social media to market your website, there is a lot that you can do with social media pages. You may not need your own website but you definitely need your own social media pages. You can create free social pages with Facebook, Linkedin, Twitter, Google, and others. To develop your contacts you will need to "friend" or "connect" with people or search for those in your target market and send them requests. You can also send announcements to your entire email list, but keep in mind that it will also go to many of your personal friends and family that you may not wish to market your services to. It is a good idea to keep a separate email list for your business contacts. The social media networks are free and provide this service of sending friend or contact requests to your email list. You can also choose to pay for additional advertising, or have a professional account that will offer more services.

You can post your class schedules, articles, newsletters, special promotions, videos, audios, photos of your classes, and your students' comments about your course after they complete it. Keep in mind that people do not like to see only ads on your pages so try to make it more personal. The idea behind the success of social media, when used for marketing, is that prospective students will see your photo and regular posts and feel like they are getting to know you personally.

People are more inclined to want to do business with someone they know and trust.

Your Facebook account will be in your name but you can also open a company page in your business' name and people can have the option to "like" your page and join it. Your Linkedin network is also in your own name but you can list your company name and provide the information about yourself and your company. With your Twitter account you can join with other people who have similar interests. You can tweet events or words of wisdom as often as you like. You can also join support groups on many of the social networks that have discussions on various topics and through your comments gain notoriety in your field.

- **YouTube videos:** You can set up a YouTube channel and upload your videos. You can upload videos of your classes, interviews, or lectures that you have given. It is easy for you to film your own video right on your PC, or ask a friend to assist you, and upload that to Youtube. You will receive memberships to your Youtube channel from those who like your videos and they will receive a notice when your new videos are posted. You can also join other Youtube channels of like interest and ask them to reciprocate by joining yours. This is free advertising so it is good to take advantage of it. You can also post your videos on your website and social media pages.

- **Internet search engines:** If you have a website or social media business page you can advertise using the pay-per-click ads by Google, Yahoo, and/or, Facebook ads. They all offer ads specifically for your location and target markets. You can bid for your placement of each key word and select your location. With Facebook ads you can choose the target audience you would like to reach and choose to direct them to your website or Facebook business page. You can set a maximum amount that you wish to spend per day so that you don't go over your budget. Your website can also have meta-tags (keywords) in order for the search engines to list your website for free.

- **Writing articles and blogging:** There are many newspapers, local magazines and e-newsletters that are always looking for good, relevant articles. Call or email them first to find out the type of article they prefer and what theme to write about. You can start your own free blog using googleblog.blogspot.com. Then you can post your articles, poems, and photos of interest.

- **Press releases:** TV, radio, and articles written about you and your services: This is an extremely effective method. You can email press releases to your local newspapers, online newspapers, magazines, TV and/or radio stations that may have shows on alternative or complimentary medicine, yoga, meditation and health, and tell them about your background, the classes you are offering, or your new events or future lectures or interviews. Maybe you can find a freelance writer interested in writing an article on meditation featuring you as an expert. This will be very helpful in bringing you name recognition and many potential students with phone or email you.

  Be sure to collect the email addresses of everyone who contacts you so you can send them regular announcement of your upcoming classes and seminars. Again, repeat exposure to many people telling them about the classes is essential.

- **Showing your ripe tomato:** This is the most effective method. When a tomato is red and fully ripe but not too soft, and it is on the shelf in clear view, it doesn't need any other advertising to say "buy me, buy me!" It is so attractive that anyone seeing it will buy it. In the same way, if you are living the result of your meditation practice and emanating peacefulness, people will experience this through your presence. Then your only job is to tell them what you have to offer. This can't be stressed enough. People will only know how they can benefit from what you have to offer if you tell them. Your best marketing tool then is your own power of expression. Don't waste your time on people who aren't interested or people who don't ask you about what you are doing. However, for those who do ask, or who show any interest, be sure to engage them in a conversation which will allow them to feel the unity that you are projecting and allow them to feel through you the serenity that you have achieved.

- **Press releases and articles written about you and your services:** This is an extremely effective method. You can mail press releases to your local paper and tell them about your background what you are now offering, or anything new that you are doing. If you can find a writer willing to write an article on meditation, and the benefits of your classes, that would be even better.

- **Word of mouth:** Direct referral of friends or relatives by your present students is the most effective method for your classes to flourish. Other professionals will also refer potential students to you when they see the benefits that their clients have received from your classes. A steady flow of students through this method will take some time to develop. Therefore, you must also use the other methods listed above. As your students will benefit tremendously from the techniques and life skills that you teach them, they will be inspired to tell those close to them. Even if they say nothing, their friends will observe the transformation in them and begin to ask them what they have done. Also, as you will always show genuine positive regard, understanding and compassion for all of your students and prospective students, and as you see and know them as your own Self, they will continually refer their friends and relatives to you. It is helpful to remind your students that you greatly appreciate their referral to interested friends so that many more people can benefit from your classes.

B. **The worst methods of advertising:** The following are methods which will not be that cost effective, as they require too much cost outlay for the amount of return. Unless you have large sums of money to market yourself, I would suggest avoiding these:

- **Large circulation newspapers ads:** These ads are costly and will reach many people who are not in your target market.

Unless you are engaging in a wide-spread and well-funded business and you can afford large ads on a regular basis, this method is not recommended. On the other hand, it would be very effective if the newspaper would write an article about you.

- **Random distribution of large quantities of your brochure:** You should have a brochure that you can mail or email and give to interested people who call you, click on your website, or who pick one up at an office or health food store. (See brochure copy in sample handbook.) Unless you have a lot of advertising dollars to spend, it is not a good idea to send them out to other people's mailing lists or to buy opt-in email lists that are expensive and can appear like spam.

- **Talks to diverse groups:** Although speaking to groups that are interested in this subject can be valuable, giving talks to large groups with varied interests may not be the most effective way to use your time. If you do give talks to interested groups, make sure you have your registration form for your next series of classes, and encourage them to register in order to receive the benefits that you are sharing with them.

- **Let someone who doesn't know you do it:** If you are giving a class at someone else's office, e.g. chiropractor or health center, it is important that you give a talk to the staff and inform them of what the course will be like so they can refer people. You should also have a phone number where people can call you for more information, as making contact with you and hearing your supportive and joyful presence will be the best way to encourage people to register.

4. **What to charge for classes:** This can be based on whatever the going rate is in your area. Do not undercharge as that will make your program less valuable. I recommend teaching a series of classes as opposed to just one class at a time. People need to commit to complete the entire program to get the maximum benefit. Without that commitment and payment in advance for a series of classes, it is much easier for them to drop out prematurely. There is a wide range of costs for meditation

programs: Some systems charge $600.00 for their course with a lifetime membership (this does not include more advanced classes, which are also costly), while community centers can charge as little as $29.00 for five classes. I recommend approximately $75.00-$95.00 for 4-5 class sessions. This makes it affordable and easy for someone to register. You then can offer more advanced classes for them to continue with. For private instruction you can charge $80.00-$150.00 per session, and more if you go to their home or office. If you are already a psychotherapist, or are conducting individual sessions with clients, you can include meditation as one of the techniques that you use in your therapeutic treatment. You, therefore, may be able to received third party reimbursement. If you teach classes it can be a means for you to charge lower fees per client as it can be done in a large group. This can enable you to attract privately paying clients and not be as dependent on managed care or insurance reimbursement.

5. **How to overcome aversion to promoting yourself:** This used to be a difficult area for me. I had the mistaken belief that I should not have to sell this to anyone and people should just come on their own. I learned that with this attitude no one would know what I had to offer. As I was offering the most valuable teachings that anyone could offer, how were people going to know unless I told them? You can have a ripe tomato but if you don't put it in the market where people can see it then no one can buy it. In the same way, if you have benefited tremendously from your meditation practice but you don't reveal your secrets to anyone as to how they may also get this benefit, how will they find out?

Therefore, it is essential that you talk to people about your programs. If you are already in a helping profession you can find out what interests your patients or clients. If you think they would be interested, let them know about it. You must develop the perspective and complete confidence that what you have to offer is the most beneficial. Proselytizing is not recommended. Don't bother with people who are not interested; there are enough people who are. You don't have to sound like an evangelist; just share yourself. You can let people know that you are educating them about meditation only so that they can also receive the benefit. You are not selling them anything or trying to persuade them or convince them of anything. If you are a ripe tomato, or you are a living example of the benefits of meditation, they will experience your love, peaceful nature, appreciation and highest knowledge. Then you just have to tell them when your classes are and give them a brochure so they will know where to find you.

6. **Answering phone calls and emails:** If you implement the best methods that I have suggested, you should receive a steady stream of phone calls and emails inquiring about your classes. The following is a good format for how to answer people who contact you by telephone.

   A. **Ask them if they have any experience of meditation:** This will let you know what their level of understanding is before giving them information.

   B. **Tell them how they will benefit before giving them the price:** What good is it for them to know how much the course costs if they don't know the benefits they will receive? Imagine a restaurant advertising food for $10.00 and not telling you what kind of restaurant it is or what the dinner includes. There is a wide range of what you can get for your money, and without that knowledge price is meaningless.

   C. **Registration information:** Tell them you will mail or email them a brochure and that it has the information on it. Tell them what the advantage will be for advanced registration.

   D. **Tuition:** Explain the time of each class and the number of sessions in the series. If there is still objection to the price, find out what it is; then you can address it. You can stress that making an investment in themselves and in their own education will last a lifetime, whereas spending money on movies and dinner is temporal. Mention that a manual will be included for their home use.

   E. **Money-back guarantee:** As you want everyone to feel satisfied that they are getting what you told them they would, why not offer a money-back guarantee? This way they can feel comfortable that if they don't like it, it won't cost them anything and they will feel easier about prepaying for the course. You can tell them if they are not satisfied after taking the first class of the series you will return their money for the entire course. If they have paid in advance then they are somewhat committed and not likely to ask for a refund. If they want a refund you should give it to them because it is good public relations as they will leave with positive feelings towards you.

7. **How to encourage students to continue:** During the series it is important to keep stressing the necessity of continuing their practice and the benefit of having a group to meditate with and a teacher to keep guiding them on their path.

   A. **Offer an incentive:** In the second-to-last class of the series and in the last class of the series you can offer them a reduced rate if they sign up for additional classes. Since they will be in a great space from enjoying the classes and experiencing the benefits first-hand, that is the best time to make sure they commit to additional classes.

   B. **New course topics:** Describe the more advanced classes and what they will learn from continuing, giving them an option of various classes that focus on different topics. This will help inspire them to continue and will help you if you want to make your teaching into a full-time career, holding several classes per week.

GLOSSARY OF SANSKRIT TERMS

Aabhyantar vritti	When the praan flows in
Aasan	Seat, posture
Abhinivaysh	Fear of death
Ahankaar	Ego or sense of individual "I"
Amamram hum	I am immortal
Ashtang yog	The eight-part practice of *Yog*
Asmitaa	"I" separate from Self
Avidyaa	Ignorance of the Self
Ayurved	Science of life, system of Indian medicine
Baahya vritti	When the *praan* flows out
Bhagavad Gita	The song of God, an ancient text
Baikhari vaani	Repeating the mantra and hearing it silently inside your head or ear
Buddhi	Intellect
Chit	Consciousness
Chitt	Mind-lake; the sense of duality
Darshan	Vision
Dhaarnaa	Concentration on one point
Dhyaan	Meditation or unbroken one-pointed-ness
Dhyaan yog	Path to unity using meditation
Dwaysh	Aversion
Gyaan yog	Path to Knowledge of Oneness
Hatha yog	Practice of physical postures
Kaivalya	Perfect Self-realization
Klaysh	Obstacles
Madhyamaa vaani	Mantra is spoken inside your mind and then it is permeating your mind
Madhuram hum	I am blissful
Manas	Mind
Mantra	Sound formula to release the mind, usually used in meditation
Nirbeej samaadhi	Perfect Self-realization
Nirodh	Experience of "I" and the whole

GLOSSARY OF SANSKRIT TERMS (CONTINUED)

Nishkaam karm yog	Action without attachment to the result
Niyam	Injunction for mental purification
Paraa vaani	After repeating the mantra you know that there is no time and space
Parinaam dukh	Pain felt as a direct result of an action
Pashyanti vaani	The life pulsation is felt and the mantra is spread in the whole sky or universe
Patanjali	Formulator of *yog darshan,* yoga sutras
Patanjali Yog Darshan	Vision of Oneness, according to Sage Patanjali
Praan	Life force energy
Praanaayaam	Method of realization of the vital life force, often through the breath
Pratyahaar	Stability of the mind in itself
Raag	Attraction, attachment
Raj yog	Royal path to the union of mind and Self
Saadhanaa	Spiritual practice
Saankhya yog	School of yogic science
Samaadhi	Absorption in the absolute
Sanskaar	Mental impressions
Sanskaar dukh	Pain due to memory
Shaant	Still, motionless
Siddhi	Powers
Stambh vritti	Cessation of movement of *praan*
Taap dukh	Pain due to imagination
Turiya	The fourth state of consciousness
Vritti	Mental wave or modification
Yam	Injunction for mental improvement
Yog	The path to unity consciousness

*Definitions are adapted from *Shyam Vedanant: The Philosophic Terminology of Swami Shyam* by Rhonda Himes (1987) and *Patanjali Yog Darshan* by Swami Shyam (2001).

KEY TO SANSKRIT PRONUNCIATION

The transliteration of the Sanskrit terms used in this manual has been adapted from Feinstein (1999), *Let's Learn Hindi.* I believe that this system supports a more exact pronunciation than some of the more widely used methods. The following is a short key to the often mispronounced sounds. For the full transliteration guide, please refer to the text mentioned above.

Single vowel and double vowel

The short vowel sound "a" is pronounced as the "u" in butter. The long vowel "aa" is pronounced as in father. The other vowels follow the same pattern - those that are written as a double vowel are pronounced with a longer vowel sound.

Each consonant in Sanskrit has an inherent "a" sound pronounced after it; therefore, the "a" which has been used at the end of a word in other transliteration schemes is sometimes omitted in this one. This avoids confusing it with a vowel "a" sound, such as in the word yoga which doesn't have an "a" in the Sanskrit but it is usually transliterated as "yoga." The correct pronunciation of the Sanskrit should be without a longer "a" sound such as in *yog.* However, when this word is used as an English word it will be spelled "yoga."

Aspirated sounds

The "h" after a consonant is pronounced with an extra release of breath.

REFERENCES

Barnhofer, T., Crane, C., Hargus, E., et. al. (2002). Mindfulness-based cognitive therapy as a treatment for chronic depression. *Behaviour Research And Therapy*. 47(5): 366–373.

Benson, H. (1975). *The relaxation response*. New York: Avon Books.

Benson, H. (1996). *Timeless healing*. New York: Fireside.

Berger, L. (1999). A therapy gains ground in hospitals: meditation. *New York Times*, Nov. 25.

Blumenthal, J. (2002). *American Journal of Cardiology*. Cited in *Atlantic Journal. Constitution Science News*, Jan. 16.

Bonadonna R. (2003). Meditation's impact on chronic illness. *Holistic Nurse Practisioner*. 17 (6) 309-19.

Borysenko, J. (1987). *Minding the body, mending the mind*. New York: Bantam.

Burdick, D. (2013). *Mindfulness Skills Workbook for Clinicians and Clients, 111 Tools, Techniques, Activities and Worksheets*. Eau Clarie, WI: PESI Publishing and Media.

Burdick, D. (2014). *Mindfulness Skills for Kids & Teens: A Workbook for Clinicians & Clients with 154 Tools, Techniques, Activities & Worksheets*. Eau Clarie, WI: PESI Publishing and Media.

Carlson, L. E., Beattie, T. L., et. al. (2015). Mindfulness-based cancer recovery and supportive-expressive therapy maintain telomere length relative to controls in distressed breast cancer survivors. *Cancer*. 3 (121) 476–484.

Carmody J. F, Crawford S., et. al. (2011). Mindfulness training for coping with hot flashes: results of a randomized trial. National Center for Biotechnology Information (NCBI), U.S. *National Library of Medicine. Menopause*. 18 (6): 611-20. doi: 10.1097/gme.0b013e318204a05c.

Chopra, D. (1993). *Ageless body, timeless mind*. New York: Random House.

Feinstein, C. D. (1999). *Let's learn Hindi*. New Delhi: Sterling.

Holze, B. K., Carmody, J., et. al. (2011). Mindfulness practice leads to increases in regional brain gray matter density. *Psychiatry Research: Neuroimaging.* 191(1): 36-43.

Jha, A., Baime, M., (2007). Meditation is an active and effortful process that literally changes the way the brain works. Cited in *Science Daily,* Jun. 25, 2007.

Jung, C.G. (1933). *Modern man in search of a soul.* San Diego: Harvest.

Kabat-Zinn, J. (1994). *Wherever you go there you are.* New York: Hyperion.

Kabat-Zinn, J., et al. (1992). Effectiveness of a meditation-based stress reduction program in the treatment of anxiety disorders. *American Journal of Psychiatry,* 49(7): 936-43.

Kabat-Zinn (2013). *Full Catastrophe Living: Using the Wisdom of Your Body and Mind to Face Stress, Pain, and Illness.* New York: Bantam Books.

Kuyken, W. (2008). Mindfulness Based Cognitive Therapy (MBCT) was as good or better as treatment... *Journal of Consulting and Clinical Psychology.* 76(6): 966-978.

Luders, E., Cherbuin, N., Kurth, F. (2015). Forever young(er): potential age-defying effects of long-term meditation on gray matter atrophy, *Frontiers in Psychology.* (5): 1-7. http://journal.frontiersin.org/article/10.3389/fpsyg.2014.01551/abstract

Maslow, A. (1970). *Religious values and peak experiences.* New York: Penguin Books.

Miller, J., Fletcher, K., & Kabat-Zinn, J. (1995). Three-year follow up and clinical implications of a mindfulness meditation-based stress reduction intervention in the treatment of anxiety disorders. *General Hospital Psychiatry.* 17(3): 192-200.

National Institutes of Health (1995). The integration of behavioral and relaxation approaches into the treatment of chronic pain and insomnia, Technology assessment conference statement, online Oct. 16-18, 1-34.

Ornish, D. (1990). *Dr. Dean Ornish's program for reversing heart disease.* New York: Random House.

Orme-Johnson, D.W. (1987). Medical care utilization and the Transcendental Meditation program. *Psychosomatic Medicine.* 49: 493-507.

Orme-Johnson, D.W. & Schneider, R. (1987). Reduced health care utilization in Transcendental Meditation practitioners, at the conference of the Society for Behavioral Medicine, Washington, DC.

Pelletier, K. (1977). *Mind as healer, mind as slayer.* New York: Dell Publishing.

Pitts, F.N., Jr. (1969). The biochemistry of anxiety. *Scientific American,* 220: 69-75.

Schneider Robert, (2012). Meditation may reduce death, heart attack and stroke in heart patients. American Heart Association. http://newsroom.heart.org/news/meditation-may-reduce-death-heart-240647

Selye, H. (1956). *Stress of life.* New York: McGraw-Hill.

Shannanhoff-Khalso, D. (2004). An introduction to kundalini yoga meditation techniques that are specific for the treatment of psychiatric disorders. *Journal of Alternative Complementary Medicine,* 2 (10): 91-101.

Shyam, S. (1985). *Bhagavad gita.* Delhi, India: Be All Publications.

Shyam, S. (1988). *Direction of life.* Delhi, India: Be All Publications.

Shyam. S. (2001). *Patanjali yog darshan.* Delhi, India: Be All Publications.

Sibbritt, D., et al. (2011). The prevalence and characteristics of young and mid-age women who use yoga and meditation: Results of a nationally representative survey of 19,209 Australian women. *Complementary Therapies in Medicine.* (19): 71—77.

Steiner, B. (2014). Treating chronic pain with meditation. *The Atlantic.* http://www.theatlantic.com/health/archive/2014/04/treating-chronic-pain-with-meditation/284182/

Sundquist, J. Lilja, A., Palmé, K. et. Al. (2014). Mindfulness group therapy in primary care patients with depression, anxiety and stress and adjustment disorders: randomised controlled trial. *BJ Psych.* 3(206) http://bjp.rcpsych.org/content/early/2014/11/11/bjp.bp.114.150243.article-info.

Sutkin, S. (2003). The anti-drug for anxiety. *Yoga Journal.* Mar./Apr. 108-114.

Urbanowski, F.B., & Miller, J.J., (1996). Trauma, psychotherapy, and meditation. *Journal of Transpersonal Psychology.* 28(1), 31-48.

Wells, R.E., Burch, R., Paulsen, R. H., et. al. (2014). Meditation for Migraines: A Pilot Randomized Controlled Trial. Cited in *Headache: The Journal of Head and Face Pain,* 54, (9): 1484-1495.

Wells, R.E., Yeh, G. Y., Kerr C. E., et. al., (2013). Meditation's impact on default mode network and hippocampus in mild cognitive impairment: A pilot study. *Neuroscience Letters.* 2013; 556: 15 DOI: 10.1016/j.neulet.2013.10.001.

Zeidan, F., Martucci, K.T., Kraft, R.A., et. al. (2011). Brain mechanisms supporting the modulation of pain by mindfulness meditation. *The Journal of Neuroscience,* 6 April 2011, 31(14): 5540-5548; doi: 10.1523/JNEUROSCI.5791-10.2011

Teacher Training Quiz

If you have registered for the course and receive 70% correct or more on this quiz, you will receive a Certificate of Achievement by email within 14 days.

To take this quiz and complete your course evaluation online, for your records, first mark your answers below. Then proceed to the link given in your registration confirmation email. Please email us if you require further assistance. quiz@transformationmeditation.com

Chapter 1

1. What is the biggest misconception about meditation?

a. it is easy	b. you should not have any thoughts
c. you will fall asleep	d. you will become happy

2. Deepak Chopra, the famous Ayurvedic physican, said...

a. our physical bodies are 99.9% space	b. Ayurvedic medicine is better than Western medicine
c. meditation cures illness	d. learning creates earning

3. What is the original text of yogic meditation philosophy and practice?

a. Patanjali Yog Darshan	b. Deepak Chopra
c. Dalai Lama	d. Yogananda

Chapter 2

4. Abraham Maslow called an exalted state...

a. the zone	b. a peak or transcendent experience
c. the true state	d. the fourth state

5. What do many people incorrectly believe will bring lasting happiness?

a. the fulfillment of a desire	b. meditation
c. money	d. a and c

Chapter 3

6. Carl Jung said...

a. psychotherapy only works for some people	b. we cannot keep up with the demand of health care professionals to learn this
c. if you want to execute a desire then release the power within yourself	d. Western developments are only a beginner's attempt compared to what is immemorial in the East

7. What are the causes of pain due to action, according to Patanjali?

a. something once enjoyable is no longer	b. the memory of something that you liked that you no longer have
c. fearing losing something you enjoy	d. a, b and c

Chapter 4

8. According to the science of meditation, what are three of the parts of the mind?

a. collection of data, sense of "I" ness, intellect	b. ego, id, superego
b. thought, form and space	d. movement, memory, intuition

9. What are the four states of consciousness?

a. dream, awake, daydream, sleep	b. conscious, unconscious, dream, meditative state
c. waking, dreaming, deep sleep, meditative state	d. waking, unconscious, sleep, beta

Chapter 5

10. According to psychologists when can you have a peak experience?

a. when you get a promotion	b. when you are in love
c. when you are in nature	d. both b and c

11. What does the Bhagavad Gita say about the Self?

a. it is limited	b. It can't be cut by weapons, burnt by fire, or wet by water, or dried by the wind
c. It is indestructible	d. both b and c

Chapter 6

12. The following is/are included in the eight limbs of yoga...

a. purification of the mind	b. breathing techniques
c. meditation	d. a, b and c

13. The stages of meditation are...

a. inquiry into an object, inquiry into a thought	b. bliss, I alone am, without a seed
c. inner and outer	d. both a and b

Chapter 7

14. What is the most important obstacle to Self-realization?

a. ignorance of the Self	b. fear of speaking
c. sleeping too much	d. overeating

15. Attachment and aversion are...

a. obstacles to Self-realization	b. neutralized through meditation
c. based on dependency	d. a, b and c

16. What troubles can you expect during your meditation practice?

a. lack of interest	b. hunger
c. doubt	d. both a and c

Chapter 8

17. Waves are to the ocean as thoughts are to ...

a. Pure Consciousness	b. dreams
c. mind	d. waking state

18. The nature of desire is that...

a. it brings total freedom and happiness	b. It gets you out of bed in the morning
c. it is wrong	d. both a and b

19. What factors can affect your health?

a. identified thoughts	b. heredity
c. major stressors	d. a, b and c

Chapter 9

20. Hans Selye (1956) said that stress is...

a. not necessary for life	b. necessary to life and all living things
c. necessary for procreation and self preservation	d. both b and c

21. According to Pelletier (1977), standard medical textbooks attribute what percentage of illness to be stress-related?

a. 5-10%	b. 50-80%
c. 90-100%	d. 40-60%

22. Hans Selye (1956) calls ordinary diseases...

a. diseases of adaptation	b. not necessary
c. developmental	d. somatic

23. The fight-or-flight response refers to...

a. desire to be in control	b. feeling like you want to fight or run away in a stressful situation
c. secretion of adrenaline and epinephrin; also increased blood pressure and heart rate.	d. both b and c

24. Herbert Benson (1975) coined the term the "Relaxation Response" which...

a. increases your oxygen consumption and limits your alpha waves	b. counteracts the effects of the fight-or-flight response
c. lowers heart rate and blood pressure	d. both b and c

Chapter 10

25. According to Benson (1996), the "Relaxation Response" can be brought about by...

a. meditation	b. autogenic training
c. jogging	d. a, b and c

26. The term "remembered wellness" includes...

a. feeling good	b. the placebo effect
c. affirmative beliefs healing us	d. b and c

27. The components of "remembered wellness" are...

a. belief and expectancy on the part of the patient	b. belief and expectancy on the part of the caregiver
c. non-competition	d. a and b

28. Calson (2015) found that breast cancer survivors...

a. couldn't meditate	b. benefited from stress reduction
c. were unhappy in groups	d. disliked meditation

29. According to Professor Mark Williams (2008) Mindfulness-Based Cognitive Therapy (MBCT) helps people to...

a. increase survival	b. stay well after depression
c. eat healthier	d. remain depressed

30. Praying for others was shown by R. C. Byrd to...

a. not help people	b. reduce cardiac arrests
c. increase pneumonia	d. make people happy

Chapter 11

31. Mindfulness Meditation is about...

a. wakefulness and being present to the moment	b. changing your thoughts
c. controlling your thoughts	d. thinking positively

32. Jon Kabat-Zinn (1994) says that rather than doing practice, it might be better said that...

a. the practice is doing you	b. the practice is difficult
c. the practice is easy	d. the practice doesn't matter

33. In a group stress-reduction program, Kabat-Zinn (1992) found that Mindfulness Meditation...

a. reduces symptoms of anxiety and panic	b. makes people sleep more
c. increases longevity	d. does not improve symptoms of anxiety

Chapter 12

34. According to the National Institutes of Health Technology Assessment Conference in 1995, chronic pain and insomnia can be helped by...

a. sleep	b. relaxation and behavior therapies
c. self-actualization	d. dialogue

35. Health statistics kept on two thousand Transcendental Meditation meditators showed...

a. increased heart rates	b. less productivity
c. half the doctors' visits and hospitalizations	d. more headaches

36. Dr. Dean Ornish (1990) recommends the following to help reverse heart disease...

a. exercise	b. low fat diet
c. meditation and yoga	d. a, b and c

37. Mindfulness Meditation combined with psychotherapy, according to Urbanowski, can...

a. decrease mental health care utilization	b. enhance the psychotherapeutic process
c. decrease ego strength	d. both a and b

38. The National Institutes of Health were given 10 million dollars a year for five years to...

a. disprove the benefits of meditation	b. discover new methods of meditation
c. expand a network of body-mind research centers	d. none of these

Chapter 14

39. The greatest fear people have has been shown to be ...

a. death	b. a fatal illness
c. public speaking	d. pain from an accident

40. What is the purpose of communication according to Shyam?

a. to make your point	b. to be happy
c. to please one another	d. to convey important information

41. How can you not communicate only for the sake of your ego?

a. be established in your blissful nature	b. close your eyes
c. look the person in the eye	d. stand straight

42. What should you do if your student asks you a confrontational question?

a. defend yourself	b. appreciate their perspective and point of view
c. ignore it	d. ask them to leave

Chapter 15

43. Diaphragmatic breathing ...

a. is done automatically by everyone	b. expands the abdomen in order for one to take in more oxygen
c. reverses the stress response	d. b and c

44. The four stages of mantra meditation are...

a. sound is heard in ears, sound is spoken inside the mind, life pulsation is felt, no time and space exist to describe the experience	b. singing, saying, hearing and internalizing
c. outside, inside, concentration, thougtless	d. awareness, consciousness, helpfulness and knowledge

Chapter 16

45. Mantra means?

a. man and trees	b. song
c. mind release	d. a and b

46. The Knower is...

a. the mind	b. the true Self
c. the body	d. the objects

Chapter 17

47. "Showing your ripe tomato" refers to...

a. using a lot of makeup	b. going to many places
c. living the result of your own meditation	d. talking to everyone about meditation

48. What are the best ways to advertise?

a. community calendar announcements	b. develop your own mailing list
c. send out thousands of brochures	d. both a and b

49. How can you best answer phone calls from people interested in meditation classes?

a. tell them the benefits first	b. tell them the cost first
c. tell them how to meditate	d. call them back later

50. How can you inspire your students to continue meditation practice?

a. offer an incentive	b. tell them the new course topics
c. ask them to commit to the next series	d. a, b and c

COURSE EVALUATION FORM

Name_____   Date_____

Please rate the program according to the following criteria:
(5= excellent 4= good 3= satisfactory 2= needs improvement 1= poor)

	5	4	3	2	1
1. Quality of writing					
2. Ease of use					
3. Value of information					
4. Relevance to practice					
5. Quality of manuals and recordings					
6. Price of program					
7. Punctuality of delivery					
8. Overall quality of program					

9. What are the primary reasons for your enrolling in this practice?

Interest in the subject _____ Personal growth _____

Earning credits_____ Teaching _____ Other_____

10. Would you like additional courses on similar topics? _____

If yes, check which ones: Breathing techniques _____

*Patanjali Yog Darshan*_____ *Bhagavad Gita* _____

Other methods of meditation _____Advanced training _____

11. Additional Comments:_____

_____

_____

Instructions: To take this Quiz and complete the Course Evaluation Form online, use the link provided in your registration confirmation email or email us for the link at quiz@transformationmeditation.com

TRANSFORMATION MEDITATION

Handouts and Samples Manual

Sherrie Wade

TRANSFORMATION MEDITATION

HOME-STUDY TEACHER TRAINING
HANDOUTS AND SAMPLES MANUAL

By Sherrie Wade, M.A.
Licensed Mental Health Counselor (#MH3015)
National Certified Counselor

Includes: Handouts for the five-class series for foundation and intermediate level courses, sample brochure, letters and marketing materials.

This Handouts and Samples Manual can be used along with the Teacher Training Instruction Manual and the two audio recordings as part of the Transformation Meditation Teacher Training Course.

If you have purchased this home-study course manual but have not registered for the Teacher Training Course, you can do so online at **www.transformationmeditation.com** and become eligible for your Certificate of Achievement and professional continuing education units (where applicable.)

Table of Contents

Introduction

This Teacher Training Handouts and Samples Manual was compiled for your use in your classes and for your promotional needs. It includes printed materials that you can copy in order to create two handout manuals to give to your students. The first one is for the Foundation Series and the second one is for the intermediate course. Many of the writings in the Teacher Training Instruction Manual can also be copied and given to your students as writings that pertain to the particular subject that you are teaching in each class. Each handout manual can be placed in a folder and given to the students at the first class in the series. For the five-session Foundation Series there are one or more printed sheets in the manual that can be used for each class in the series. Students can be asked to bring the manual to each class. If they would like to read ahead, they should be made aware that they may not understand everything and that is fine, as you will be covering the material in future classes.

This Handouts and Samples Manual also includes samples of marketing materials, such as brochures, press releases, a newspaper column and letters. Those who have registered for and completed the Transformation Meditation Home-Study Teacher Training Course may copy any of these materials for their use in teaching Transformation Meditation. If you want to promote a series of classes for yourself, you can use the guidelines that follow: Each prospective student who calls for information about your classes should be placed on a mailing list. The date they called and notes regarding their interests and meditation experience should be recorded. Then you should send them a brochure for the next available course, along with a cover letter and the commonly-asked question sheet. The brochure should include all the registration information. If they have e-mail you can also send them a follow-up e-mail, but you might like to send the brochure by mail as it can be printed on nice paper and they will have a hard copy at hand as well as the e-mail. If they do not attend the next available course, you can keep their name on the list and send them a brochure for future classes.

The teacher training audio recording that you receive with this course will guide you in explaining each handout that goes with each class in the series. The second audio recording, Infinite Peace, will guide you in leading the meditations and the deep relaxation. This recording can also be ordered and resold to your students to enable them to practice at home. You can also record your own tape or CD, if you like, to sell to them for home use.

These course materials, teaching aids and promotional materials have been used for many years with great success. Most of those who attended these classes expressed that their lives were greatly enriched and improved. You can read some of the comments that were made by graduating students in the letters enclosed. Best of luck to you in providing the most comprehensive, thorough, rewarding and fun class for your students. If you have any questions on how to conduct these sessions please feel free to send an e-mail; your questions will be answered in a timely fashion.

Transformation Meditation

Foundation Series Handout Manual

The following pages, 140-152, may be copied and used to help you develop a handout manual to give to your students. You can make your personalized cover page and then copy these pages, or adapt them, to meet your own individual needs.

Meditation and Relaxation Training Benefits

(Based on recent research)

Psychological/Emotional Benefits:

- Reduces anxiety and eliminates phobias
- Reduces stress and reverses the fight-or-flight reaction
- Creates a sense of inner peace and calm
- Accelerates the psychotherapeutic process
- Reduces the use of prescription drugs
- Reduces the use of alcohol and other substances
- Useful in smoking and weight reduction programs
- Improves grades at school

Physical Health Benefits:

- Improvement for asthma sufferers
- Strengthens the immune system and reduces viruses
- Reduces cardiovascular problems
- Increases blood flow to the heart
- Improvement for diabetics
- Increases athletic performance
- Reduces chronic pain
- Lowers blood pressure
- Lengthens life span

Work-Related Benefits:

- Reduces sick days
- Improves productivity
- Improves work performance
- Decreases use of employee insurance benefits
- Stimulates creativity
- Increases job satisfaction
- Improves relationships with supervisors and co-workers

How Stress Can Affect YOU

When you are in a stressful situation the body responds with the

Fight-or-flight response:

1. The sympathetic nervous system stimulates receptors in the heart that make it beat faster and harder, preparing you to fight or run away. This can cause the coronary arteries to constrict.

2. The brain causes other organs such as the adrenal glands to secrete stress hormones such as adrenaline, and steroids such as cortisol, which circulate in the blood until they reach the heart.

A series of physiological reactions occurs:

1. The muscles contract, helping to fortify the body's armor to help protect it from injury.

2. The metabolism speeds up the heart rate and the amount of blood pumped with each beat increases.

3. Breathing increases, providing more oxygen, to do battle or run from the danger.

4. The digestive system shuts down, diverting energy to the muscles that are needed in order to run.

5. Arteries in our arms and legs constrict so that less blood will be lost if you become wounded.

6. Blood clots more quickly so as not to lose blood due to injury.

Chronic stress can cause:

1. Tension, anxiety and/or depression

2. More blood clots in the arteries which reduces blood flow to the heart.

3. Arteries in the heart to constrict which can cause spasms. When a coronary artery goes into spasm it can injure the lining of the artery leading to cholesterol deposits and plaque build-up.

4. High blood pressure

5. Weakened nervous and immune system

(Adapted from *Dr. Dean Ornish's Program for Reversing Heart Disease*.Random House, 1990.)

What is Meditation?

By Sherrie Wade, M.A.

Meditation is the process of experiencing a state of pure awareness. Through calming the mind and emotions you can experience a state of peace and tranquility. Meditation is a simple technique that can be learned in a few minutes. To master it requires continued practice, guidance and mature knowledge of the process.

According to the science of meditation, optimum existence is experienced when even the most subtle aspect of your thought leads you to the experience of peace or harmony. Subtle forms of thought are called waves of perception. Through the practice of meditation you can train yourself to de-identify with the passing thoughts or waves of perception that lead the attention towards identifying with stressful situations. Instead, you focus on the pure awareness state, also called the Knower or experiencer of thoughts. When you no longer identify or become mixed in any particular thought or physical sensation, then the space behind the thought, which is always peaceful, is experienced. This is termed by psychologists as a peak experience, the transpersonal self, and by yogic practitioners as the fourth state of consciousness.

Through the practice of meditation and the observation of your thoughts, you develop the power to discriminate between those thought that are useful and those that are not. The mind is seen as an instrument that is used to perceive the world. You can develop the power to observe your mental functioning and maintain the awareness that you are the observer of your mind. You can then choose which thoughts to identify with and which ones to act on, de-identifying with irrational or destructive thoughts or beliefs. These negative thoughts or waves of perception can be allowed to pass without holding on to them, or they can be observed as if watching them on a screen. As you focus on the consciousness out of which these thoughts or waves are arising, you are led to experience the peace that is at the back of the thought.

Thoughts have certain qualities. Some thoughts produce more stress by leading the attention towards worries, doubts, fears and skepticism. Thoughts that are positive can be retained; those that are negative can be released. You do not need to stop the flow of these thoughts; they do not create any problem unless you, the Self, identifies with them.

The natural function of the mind is to think, and no thought is destructive if there is no effect from it.

Meditation allows you to spend time aware of yourself as the Self, or the Knower of all the thoughts and phenomena. From this state you can experience both negative and positive emotions and maintain the knowledge of the peaceful Self. The Knower state is always peaceful as it is the Pure Consciousness or life itself. Suffering occurs only when the Knower, forgetting its true nature, identifies with the thought of the mind and feelings of the physical body.

Meditation is known to relax the physiology and reverse the damaging effects of stress. So many people are feeling uneasy, isolated and lonely. These feelings can create tension, weaken the immune system and cause disease. The immune system is strengthened and healing is accelerated by developing a positive attitude and visualization of health. Using the Transformation Meditation system of meditation, the mind is trained to continuously focus on the life force or Pure Consciousness, even before the thought arises. In this way, the problem of having a negative attitude or belief system is taken care of at its source. This can save a lot of time and the effort of sorting through and trying to change an infinite number of negative thoughts and beliefs. In fact, it takes care of the problem before it even arises by focusing the attention at the source of the thought, or the Pure Consciousness state.

Breathing Techniques - *Praanaayaam*

Deep Abdominal Breathing

1. Exhale all the breath while gently pulling in the abdomen.

2. Begin inhaling while puffing out the abdomen.

3. Gently bring the breath upwards, allowing the rib cage to move to the side, then continue bringing the breath up, thus expanding the chest.

4. Slowly begin to exhale the breath reversing this process, exhaling from the chest, allowing the rib cage and then the abdomen to gently go down.

BENEFITS:

Deep abdominal breathing reverses the stress reaction by providing more oxygenation of the blood resulting in greater relaxation, better emotional balance and control, greater mental clarity and acuity, and greatly improved general health. It switches on the parasympathetic part of the involuntary nervous system which allows the system to rest, relax and repair. Your lung capacity will gradually increase so you will become less winded by exertion.

Alternate-Nostril Breathing

1. Making a gentle fist with the right hand, extend the thumb and the last two fingers, leaving a space for the nose.

2. With the thumb, close off the right nostril and exhale through the left.

3. Using the deep abdominal breathing, inhale through the left nostril then close it off with the last two fingers and exhale through the right nostril. Continue by inhaling through the right nostril, closing it off and exhaling through the left.

BENEFITS:

Alternate-nostril breathing can help soothe, purify and strengthen the nervous system. It can help you to develop control of your body, mind and emotions. It also helps to increase mental alertness, cleanse and open the nasal passages, normalize the metabolic process and combat the overall detrimental effects of stress.

This Is Meditation

Eight Steps to Meditation Practice

1. Sit with your back comfortably straight, your head and neck aligned with the spine as much as possible.

2. Gently close your eyes.

3. Notice the space that you see in front of your closed eyes.

4. Make an imaginary circle in the middle of the space, the circumference of which is according to your own imagination.

5. From the center of the circle, coming as if to your eyes, begin to speak the mantra, *Amaram Hum Madhuram Hum*, I am Immortal I am blissful.

6. Focus your attention on the last syllable of each word spoken in order to continue focusing the attention on the first syllable of the next word. Continue this type of repetition with one-pointedness.

7. Be aware of the Knower who knows how to speak the mantra, how to listen to the words in silence, and how to know the meaning contained in these words.

8. During this period, thoughts will come, arise, stay or go away. You remain neutral to them and non-dealing with them. Your attention goes to focus on the Knower, realizing that the Knower is Pure Consciousness, Pure Existence and Bliss. Continue meditating and holding this realization for a few minutes, considering that this Self or I or Knower is the source, everything, everywhere.

BENEFITS:

Reverses the fight-or-flight (stress) reaction; helps lower blood pressure and cholesterol levels; reduces the heart rate and the oxygen requirement of the body by 10-20% in the first 3 minutes (this is also an effect produced by medication to lower high blood pressure) without the side effects of medication; increases awareness and alertness; unfolds a state of Oneness and allows you to experience unity with your self and your world.

How to Transform Tension and Stress into Relaxation and Ease

1. When you are experiencing a situation in which you feel tension and unpleasant emotions, ask yourself the question, in what way would I like this situation to be different?

2. When you notice you are feeling tense, then watch the tension as it is approaching from the distance. Once it has come, accept it. Do not try to push it away or suppress it or get angry at yourself for reacting, because that will make you more tense. Just recognize and observe what you are feeling and allow yourself to experience the symptoms in your body.

3. Now, begin to breathe using the abdominal breathing technique, slowly and deeply. As you change your breathing pattern, notice that you can begin to relax and change your thinking pattern. The breath is very closely connected to your mind and emotions. Check your body and see if there is any tension in your back, neck or shoulders; if so, take a deep breath and consciously give yourself the message to relax that area of your body.

4. Notice if you want to fight, argue or run from the situation and then follow the next steps to begin to change your thinking about the situation.

5. Recognize what you are telling yourself that you want from the situation. If there is anything that you can practically do to change the situation then decide to do it; if not, then you must accept what is actually happening rather then trying to fight it mentally and emotionally. Give yourself the message that, as there is nothing you can do to change it, there is no point in having your mind dwell on it.

6. To stop dwelling on useless thoughts, you can elicit the relaxation response by placing you attention on the breath and slowing down the number of breaths you take per minute. Then start repeating the mantra, allowing the thoughts to come and go; then place your attention on the observer of the thoughts and gently bring the attention back to the breath or mantra whenever it gets involved in the thoughts.

The De-identification Process

How To Stop Worrying and Enjoy Your Life

Six Steps to Freedom from Disturbing
Thoughts and Feelings

1. Sit in a quiet place, close your eyes and begin to relax your body. (You can use a breathing technique or the second part of the deep relaxation exercise.)

2. Begin to observe your mind and your thoughts, noticing how certain thoughts keep repeating or carrying your attention into a pattern of worries or fears.

3. Notice that if you put your attention on the pause after one thought and before the next one, you experience a brief moment of peace or freedom from the effect of the thought.

4. Repeat the mantra, noticing how other thoughts come and go and you as the master of your mind can choose to put your attention on the mantra instead of paying attention to the thoughts.

5. Be aware that you are the Knower or observer of your mind and thoughts and begin to become aware of yourself as the Knower unmixed with the thoughts.

6. Whenever you notice that you have become mixed with a thought, just gently remind yourself to again repeat the mantra and be aware of yourself as the Knower.

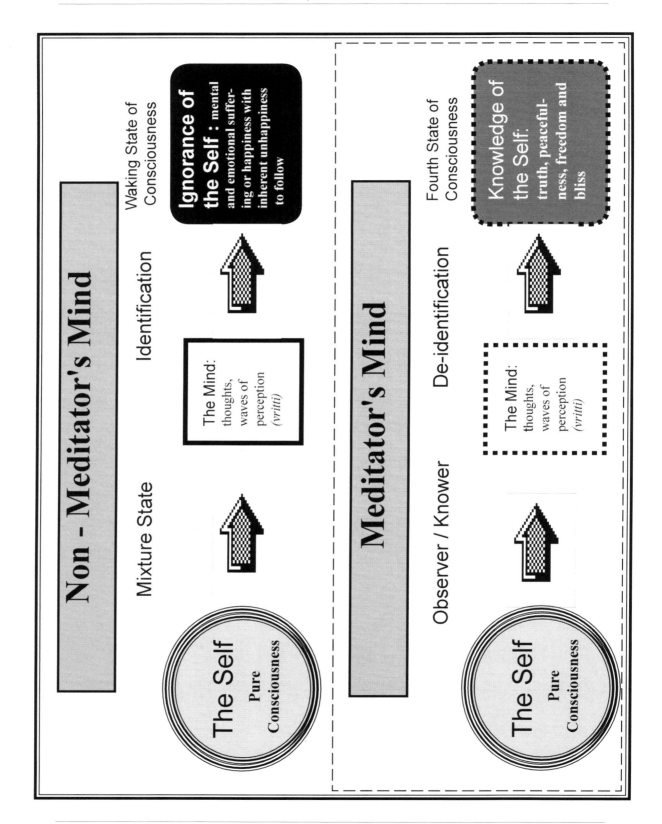

Non - Meditator's Mind

Waking State of Consciousness

Ignorance of the Self : mental and emotional suffering or happiness with inherent unhappiness to follow

Identification

The Mind: thoughts, waves of perception (*vritti*)

Mixture State

The Self
Pure Consciousness

Meditator's Mind

Fourth State of Consciousness

Knowledge of the Self: truth, peacefulness, freedom and bliss

De-identification

The Mind: thoughts, waves of perception (*vritti*)

Observer / Knower

The Self
Pure Consciousness

Various Meditation Techniques

There are many variations of the techniques of meditation that you may use. The following is a list of a few of them. Remember while practicing any meditation technique that thoughts are not a problem to you, the meditator. You can just watch them and know they are waves of perception that arise, stay and then pass. The Pure Consciousness is always present and each wave is just a modification of that, just as a wave in the ocean is the same ocean water. (Also listen to the audio recording, *Infinite Peace*, for guided meditations using some of these variations.)

1. **Repeat mantra silently to yourself:** This basic mantra meditation technique should be practiced always with the awareness that you, the Knower, are repeating the mantra and then bringing your attention to the very Knower that is you.

2. **Repeat mantra and watch the pause:** Notice the quiet space between each repetition of the mantra, knowing that bliss is forever present in the pause and also at the back of all the thoughts.

3. **Repeat mantra while counting:** You can either use a set of beads called *mala* beads and on each repetition move to the next bead (similar to a rosary), or you can count after each repetition until reaching 108. This number is considered a powerful number in yogic philosophy.

4. **Repeat the mantra out loud:** This technique is referred to as chanting and can assist you in becoming relaxed and focused. It can also enhance thesilent meditation which can follow the chanting.

5. **Create you own technique:** As long as the basic elements are there you can use any object of focus, such as your breath, a candle, or a flower. At some point you can close your eyes and watch. As long as you close your eyes and are in touch with the observer or Knower, the meditation will unfold perfectly, almost by itself. You can just watch the space at the back of your closed eyes.

Sometimes the mantra will come easily and smoothly. You don't have to repeat it in the same rhythm as your breath, though it might coordinate on its own. After some time, you may get tired of repeating it. Then you can shorten the words or just continue by watching the space that has unfolded. The mantra is a tool to get you to know the space. Once you are there, experiencing a state of peace or bliss, just enjoy! (Also see "This is Meditation," in your manual.)

Progressive Deep Relaxation

(To be read slowly out loud by a teacher or friend)

Relax on your back, arms at your side, palms turned up toward the ceiling, for deep relaxation. You will be alternately contracting and then relaxing each part of the body.

Bring the awareness to the right foot and leg - stretch out the leg, squeezing it tight, raise it one foot off the floor - RELEASE. (Repeat for the left leg.) Roll the ankles from side-to-side and relax the legs.

Bring the awareness to the right arm - stretch out the arm, the fingers, making a fist, raise it one foot off the ground - squeeze tight - RELEASE. (Repeat for left arm.) Roll the wrists and relax them..

Squeeze in the buttocks, pulling in the anus muscles - tight! - RELEASE.

Inhale, puffing out the lower abdomen. On the signal we will let the breath gush out of an open mouth. Open - RELEASE. Inhale, allow the air to come up into the chest - open the mouth - RELEASE.

Keeping the arms in place on the floor, curl the shoulders up in front of you, almost bringing them together under the chin - RELEASE. Gently roll the head and neck once or twice, returning it to the balance point of the body.

Stretch out the face, open the mouth, stick out the tongue - RELEASE. Curl the face into a ball, squeeze in the lips, eyes, forehead - RELEASE.

Now that we have physically gone over the body, keeping it still, we'll have a mental check. With the mind we will go over each part of the body. If you encounter any tension, concentrate on releasing that tightness.

Bring the awareness into the toes, soles of the feet, tops of the feet, ankles, up the shins, calves (concentrating on releasing any tightness), back of the knees, knee caps, front of the thighs, back of the thighs. Bring the awareness into the fingertips, palms of the hands, back of the hands, wrists, forearms, elbows, upper arms. Bring the awareness into the lower abdomen (pelvic region), upper abdomen (rib cage), relax all internal organs.

Be aware of the buttocks (concentrating on releasing any tension), base of the spine, now coming up the spinal column vertebra by vertebra, releasing the entire back as your awareness comes up, lower, middle back, upper. Release the shoulders from the neck outward, back of the neck, head, top of the head. Bring the awareness to the throat and lips, nose, cheeks, eyes, eyelids, eyebrows, forehead.

Bring the awareness to the breath. Without controlling the breath, witness the inhalations, exhalations. Standing apart, witnessing the flow of the breath. (1 minute interval)

Bring the awareness to the mind, witness the thoughts coming into the mind, remaining a few minutes, then drifting off without your attention being carried off on a thought. Stand apart, witnessing the flow of the mind. (1 minute)

Allow the body - breath- and mind to drift off - witness the peace and tranquility - consciously witnessing the peace within. (3 to 5 minutes)

Now begin to wiggle your fingers and toes, slowly awakening the body. (pause) Begin to stretch your arms over your head and slowly stretch the entire body - legs downward along the floor and arms above your head along the floor. (pause) Release and slowly roll onto your side into the fetal position. Rest in that position for a few moments. (pause) Slowly raise up to a sitting position facing this way.

Now take in a few deep abdominal breaths. (pause) Now a few rounds of alternate nostril breathing. Now bringing the breath back to normal and sitting in silent meditation for a few minutes. As you are very relaxed after the deep relaxation, meditation will happen almost automatically by just closing your eyes and beginning a technique.

Four Stages of Mantra Meditation

The repetition of a mantra such as *Amaram Hum Madhuram Hum* is a useful technique in meditation. It is a tool that will help you to experience your own true nature. Learning new things, such as playing a musical instrument or speaking a foreign language, is often achieved through repetition. Mantra, although practiced with repetition, is not meant to be used only with unaware rote repetition. It is meant as a method of practice which brings about a power *(siddhi)* to reach the supreme state of consciousness. In this state there is silence within the mind which becomes still *(shaant)* and eventually you will merge the mind or individual awareness with the whole, which is Pure Consciousness and Knowingness. Every time you practice you obtain the result, as this fourth state of consciousness is always with you. Therefore, the practice should be done with the awareness that you are obtaining the result rather than that you will obtain it someday in the future. The following is a focus for your repetition of mantra. You can experience these stages as you progress in your meditation. Mantra should be practiced with the focus that you, the Pure Consciousness, are meditating on Pure Consciousness.

1. **The sound is heard by your ears *(baikhari vaani):*** In this stage your students can repeat or sing the mantra out loud and then hear it silently inside their head. (You can first say it out loud, having your students listen to you, and then they can join in.)

2. **The sound is spoken inside your mind *(madhyamaa vaani):*** Then you can have them repeat it silently so that it becomes more apparent that it is permeating their mind.

3. **The life pulsation is felt and the mantra is spread in the whole sky or universe *(pashyanti vaani):*** After many repetitions, one may become aware that there is no longer anybody there to perceive, as the individual awareness gets absorbed in the space.

4. **All is Pure Existence and Consciousness *(paraa vaani):*** There is no time and space, there is nothing to describe about your experience.

Through mantra our mental being becomes subtler and subtler and vaster and vaster until perfect stillness or Oneness arises.

Recommended Reading List

Benson, H. (1975). *The Relaxation Response*. New York: Avon.

Benson, H. (1996). *Timeless Healing, The Power and Biology of Belief*. New York: Fireside.

Benson, H. & Stuart, E.M. (1993). *The Wellness Book: A Comprehensive Guide to Maintaining Health and Treating Stress Related Illness*. New York: Fireside.

Borysenko, J. (1987). *Minding The Body, Mending The Mind*. New York: Bantam.

Burdick, D. (2013), *Mindfulness Skills Workbook for Clinicians and Clients, 111 Tools, Techniques, Activities and Worksheets*. Eau Clarie, WI: PESI. Publishing and Media.

Burdick, D. (2014). *Mindfulness Skills for Kids & Teens: A Workbook for Clinicians & Clients with 154 Tools, Techniques, Activities & Worksheets*. Eau Clarie, WI: PESI. Publishing and Media.

Chopra, D. (1991). *Unconditional Life*. New York: Bantom.

Eaton, R. (2003). *Essence of Patanjali Yog Sootras Course Manual*. TransformationMeditation.com

Eaton, R. (2010). *In the Stillness of Breath: Praanaayaam for Meditators*. TransformationMeditation.com

Eaton, R. (2009). *The Sootras of Patanjali Yog Darshan: Concise Rendition*. TransformationMeditation.com

Eaton, R. (2011). *Patanjali Yog Darshan: Wisdom of Meditation*. TransformationMeditation.com

Kabat-Zinn, J. (1994). *Wherever You Go There You Are: Mindfulness Meditaion in Everyday Life*. New York: Hyperion.

Kabat-Zinn (2013). *Full Catastrophe Living: Using the Wisdom of Your Body and Mind to Face Stress, Pain, and Illness*. New York: Bantam Books.

Kezwer, G. (2005). *The Essence of the Bhagavad Gita Course Manual*. Online: TransformationMeditation.com

Ornish, D. (1990). *Dr. Dean Ornish's Program For Reversing Heart Disease*. New York: Random House.

Shyam, S. (2009). *Bhagavad Gita*. Kullu, India: I.M.I*

Shyam, S (2001). *Patanjali Yog Darshan*. Delhi, India: Be All publications.*

Shyam, S. (1994). *Vision of Oneness*. India: International Meditation Institute.*

Siegel, Bernie (1986). *Love, Medicine & Miracles.* New York: Harper & Row.

Wade, A. (2009). *Himalayan Muse* CD. TransformationMeditation.com

Wade, S. (2012). *Love's Eternal Space: Enlightening Poetry.* TransformationMeditation.com

* Books by S. Shyam can be ordered through the website: www.shyamswisdom.com.

Transformation Meditation Intermediate Series

Handout Manual

The following pages, 156-163, can be used to compile a manual to give to your students for the intermediate classes. You can use these as outlines while explaining these topics in more detail to your students. You can review or add any of the writings from the first Teacher's Manual that will pertain to the subjects, as they may contain more complete explanations.

Intermediate Breathing Techniques

When one slows down the breath rate, it gives the body a profound rest and prolongs life. Count how many times you naturally breathe in one minute. You might find anywhere from fifteen to sixty breaths. Now see if you can slow it down to half that number or less without straining. Notice the immediate result that when the breath is slower the mind becomes still and naturally peaceful.

Kumbakh (Breath Retention)

1. *Baahya-Vritti Praanaayaam:* When the breath or *praan* flows out, hold it slightly longer. This allows the body to absorb the breath and spread its *praanic* energy throughout.

2. *Aabhyantar-Vritti Praanaayaam:* When the breath or *praan* flows in and is held inside the body, it gives of its power and knowledge as it is the very life force energy.

3. *Stambh-Vritti Praanaayaam:* Breathing in and out normally, one watches where the *praan* or breath stops, whether in or out. This is the natural cessation of the *praan*.

4. **Techniques combining these three types of *praanaayaam:*** Breathe in; after you inhale, hold the breath in for a few seconds. Be careful not to hold so long that you create strain. Focus the attention on the energy in the solar plexus. Then exhale as if breathing through the nose and eyes, and after all the breath is out hold it out for a few seconds longer. Focus on the energy rising up to the top of your head. Continue this for twelve times in and out.

BENEFITS:

Holding the breath resembles a deeper meditative state whereby the breath becomes very shallow as your body's oxygen requirement is reduced so much that you hardly need any more oxygen to sustain the physical system. Therefore, your heart, lungs and all the body's systems get a profound rest. This technique also raises the praan (vital life force energy) to the higher energy centers in the body.

* Please Note: These techniques are meant to be done very gently or, rather than creating the desired benefits, you will strain and create uneasiness in your nervous system. More isn't better when you are practicing praanaayaam. Just do as much as feels comfortable.

The State of Yog (Union with the Self)

YOGASH CHITT VRITTI NIRODHAH

The general sign of the state of *yog* is described. The state of *yog* is realized in that *chitt* or mind in which the sense of identification with *vrittis* or waves of perception has ceased to arise. The waves of perception, or thoughts, that flow outwards are brought back to the source or original state of motionlessness so that the ocean of the mind remains without the slightest ripple. This state of motionlessness is called *nirodh*. When this state of mind appears in an individual, that person and the Absolute Existence, the *yog*, become one and the same.

It is not necessary to control the mind. One must sit in stillness and follow this practice. There should be no exertion, coercion or force of any kind, physical or mental. Just sit in stillness, allowing the body to rest in one easy posture for as long as possible. This is a formula like H$_2$0; if followed exactly, it has to bring the desired result.

Practice of the state of *yog*

You should never think that a particular form or thought should not take place, or that after having a thought it should be changed. You should sit at ease and start to perceive with closed eyes the center of the space in front of the third eye point. If you cannot perceive the center in any way, you should simply imagine such a center of space and continuously keep the attention on it for as long as your body can remain still. While engaged in this practice, the breath will come and go and thoughts will appear and disappear; but you do not pay any attention at all to these occurrences. You keep watching the center of the space, experiencing whatever varieties of change take place in it. For as long as you can imagine it, keep your attention fixed on the center. You must have patience and keep practicing with regularity. One day the center will reveal the truth of *yog* in practical form, and you will know for yourself that you have attained the *yog* state, the original and true nature of a human being's consciousness.

(Adapted from Shyam [2001], *Patanjali Yog Darshan*, Chapter 1, Verse 2.)

Four Types of Pain and Suffering

1. ***Parinaam dukh*** is when something is enjoyable but later on results in pain: for example, you overeat an assortment of wonderful foods and then right after eating you experience indigestion and reach for, "plop plop, fizz fizz, oh what a relief it is."

2. ***Sanskaar dukh*** is caused by the memory of something that you had but no longer have, such as when you break off from a relationship or lose a loved one. All human beings experience this pain.

3. ***Taap dukh*** comes when your sense of happiness is based on having something that you enjoy, but fear to lose (for example you own a beautiful home but fear you may lose your job and not be able to afford it). Also, when you are dependent on a relationship as the source of your happiness, you may fear being left alone.

4. ***Guna dukh*** is due to an imbalance in your energy which can be due to overwork, overplay, poor diet, sickness or keeping bad company. This type of pain is apparent when you feel tired or are in physical pain and you must get up and go to work.

The Eight Limbs of Yoga (*Ashtang Yog*)

Yoga practice is one, but it consists of eight limbs or parts:

1. **Injunctions for improvement of the mind *(yam):*** Non-violence, non-deception, non-stealing, non-swindling, constant action or thinking about the higher Self, and the attempt not to get attached to things.

2. **Injunctions for purification of the mind *(niyam):*** Purification of the body and mind so that no problem can arise from this quarter, taking everything as it comes and remaining happy and content, strenuous living, study for the purpose of liberation from ignorance, surrender and devotion to a higher power, and not over-indulging in sensual pleasures.

3. **Seat *(aasan):*** Unwavering sitting posture occurs when the body no longer feels pain and the mind is free from worry. This state is called perfect, easy sitting posture.

4. **Regulation of energies *(praanaayaam):*** Breath control, breathing techniques.

5. **Stability of the mind in itself *(pratyahaar):*** Control of the senses, concentration of the mind towards the source.

6. **Concentration or stability of the mind on any point in time and space *(dhaarna):*** When the mind is made to remain on one point inside or outside the body.

7. **Meditation or the unbroken flow of consciousness onto one object, person or space *(dhyaan):*** When the mind is made to stay in one place or on one object, and when the mind knows it is perceiving the object as it is and no other thought interferes at that time.

8. **The state in which the mind loses its individual awareness *(samaadhi):*** When, while meditating, there is only Space as it is, and when the mind merges and becomes perfectly dissolved into Space so that there lingers no separate idea of mind at all, then it is said that the state of *samaadhi* is taking place.

The Levels of Meditation (*Samaadhi*)

Inquiry into the object *(vitark)*

When one puts the attention on the gross form of an object.

1. Holding the name, form, and knowledge of the object.

2. The mind does not hold the name, form and knowledge of the object.

Inquiry into the thought *(vichaar)*

When the object taken for meditation is a subtle thought of a form.

1. Holding the name, form and knowledge of the thought.

2. The mind does not hold the name, form, and knowledge of the thought.

Inquiry into the bliss *(aanand)*

When one experiences a blissful state.

1. Holding the attention on the state of bliss.

2. There is no thought relating to the object or its thought form, yet the mind feels a kind of joy or peace and the awareness is held that "I am at peace."

Inquiry into the state of "I am" *(asmitaa)*

When there remains no feeling or awareness even of peacefulness or joy, yet there is awareness that "I am."

The Self being by itself all alone *(asampragyaat)*

The individual awareness merges entirely into the whole, which is absolute Pure Existence and Knowingness. Not a single wave remains, even of the kind that knows "I am."

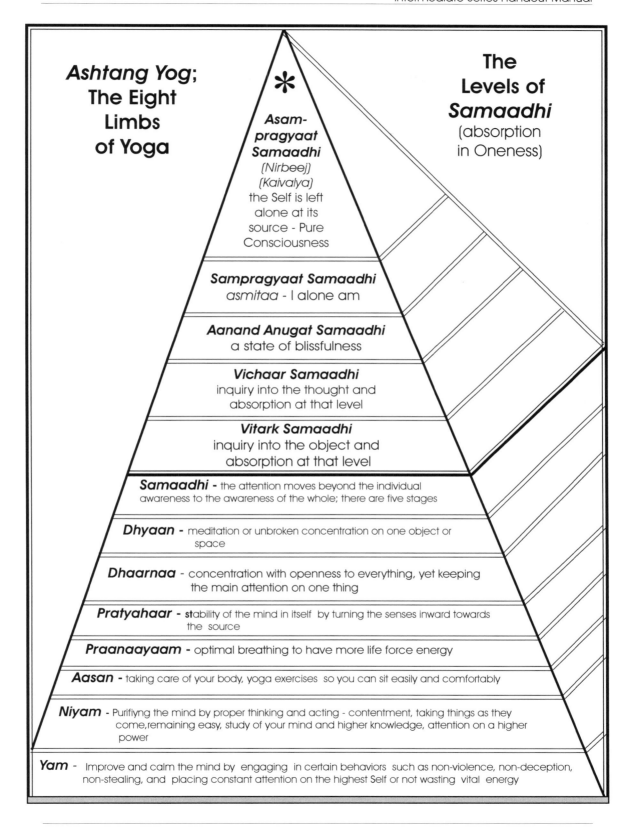

Ashtang Yog;
The Eight
Limbs
of Yoga

*

Asam-
pragyaat
Samaadhi
(Nirbeej)
(Kaivalya)
the Self is left
alone at its
source - Pure
Consciousness

The
Levels of
Samaadhi
(absorption
in Oneness)

Sampragyaat Samaadhi
asmitaa - I alone am

Aanand Anugat Samaadhi
a state of blissfulness

Vichaar Samaadhi
inquiry into the thought and
absorption at that level

Vitark Samaadhi
inquiry into the object and
absorption at that level

Samaadhi - the attention moves beyond the individual
awareness to the awareness of the whole; there are five stages

Dhyaan - meditation or unbroken concentration on one object or
space

Dhaarnaa - concentration with openness to everything, yet keeping
the main attention on one thing

Pratyahaar - stability of the mind in itself by turning the senses inward towards
the source

Praanaayaam - optimal breathing to have more life force energy

Aasan - taking care of your body, yoga exercises so you can sit easily and comfortably

Niyam - Purifiyng the mind by proper thinking and acting - contentment, taking things as they
come, remaining easy, study of your mind and higher knowledge, attention on a higher
power

Yam - Improve and calm the mind by engaging in certain behaviors such as non-violence, non-deception,
non-stealing, and placing constant attention on the highest Self or not wasting vital energy

The Obstacles (*Klaysh*) That Are Removed Through Meditation Practice

Ignorance of the Self *(avidya)*

When the true Self is forgotten and one believes himself to be only the accumulation of his mental ideas and constructs, physical body and senses, then he has fallen into the state of forgetfulness of his true Self. When one believes that permanent joy comes through the enjoyment of the sense-objects and exerts himself for possessing those objects; when he devotes his attention and energy to them and forgets that the sense-objects, no matter to what extent they are possessed and enjoyed, can never provide complete fulfillment; again treat it that ignorance of the Self has possessed him.

When a person knows that his body and ego are his real Self even though they deceive him all the time and certainly do so ultimately, know that ignorance of the Self has completely overwhelmed him.

"I" as separate *(asmitaa)*

The Seer within man is Pure Consciousness, and the mind in which the seeing and knowing occur is individual consciousness. These two, the Seer and the mind, are really strangers to each other, but due to the ignorance of the Self they become mixed together just as sugar and water may be mixed. It is at this stage of mixed understanding that the individual ego manifests and the one within forgets that he is Pure Awareness and Truth, the real Self. Instead, he knows himself as the mixture of Self and mind. Thus he becomes the "I"-consciousness of an individual man.

Attachment *(raag)*

When a person who has become ignorant of the Self, his true nature, feels happiness on account of a person, object or happening, he may begin to love that person or object, or cherish the memory of that happening. This kind of love is attachment.

Aversion; recoil from any pain-causing object *(dwaysh)*

When a person becomes insulted, hit, or troubled by a person, object, or happening, he feels pain or unhappiness. Because of this pain, he begins to hate that which he thinks caused it.

Prevailing fear of death *(abhinivaysh)*

Throughout the ages it has been observed that all sentient beings want to exist forever, from minuscule mosquitoes and gigantic animals up to the most intelligent of all, man. In the case of man, no one wishes the destruction of his own state of mind, an occurrence which must inevitably take place at the time of death. Every person and every being is afraid of death. This fear of death saturates to the very depths of man's existence.

The Troubles That May Arise
for the Practicing Mind

1. **Disease:** In the body, mind or senses.

2. **Lack of interest:** When one feels no interest in making efforts.

3. **Doubt:** A sense of weakness with respect to one's own power or uncertainty concerning the result of practice.

4. **Procrastination:** Whenever one ignores one's practice, delaying the result.

5. **Dullness, idleness:** When weakness prevails in the body due to eating wrong food, meeting with bad company, or living in a climate which creates heaviness of body or mind, and as a result one loses interest in practice.

6. **Lack of enlightenment:** Whenever the mind loses its power to perceive the reality, when it becomes caught up in hankering for the enjoyment of sense-objects and tries to attain permanent satisfaction thereby.

7. **Negative understanding:** When one begins to think that meditation is not for him and is causing him trouble.

8. **Non-attainment of the desired result:** When one practices but, due to some unknown reason, he is not progressing and so becomes discouraged.

9. **Slip of the state of mind once attained:** When one attains certain spaces of the mind, yet they vanish sometimes.

These nine troubles are removed through meditation and repetition of mantra.

(From *Patanjali Yog Darshan*, Shyam 2001)

Transformation Meditation

Samples of Marketing Materials

The following pages, 166-177, contain sample letters to students, a copy of the Transformation Meditation Foundation Series brochure, and press releases that can be sent to newspapers.

These templates can be copied and adapted for your personal use in promoting your own classes.

Sample Letter

To be sent to prospective students for Foundation Series

Date

Dear

Thank you for your interest in the Transformation Meditation Course. Transformation Meditation was developed through many years of researching many forms of meditation and the difficulties people have in understanding and learning meditation. It is a complete program that allows you to experience the meditative state easily and utilize it to improve your life.

To make this decision an easy one for you, I'm sharing with you some of the comments former students have made. This course has helped them and can help you in every area of your life. Meditation practice is the most effective way to reduce stress and anxiety, improve concentration and focus, increase productivity, improve relationships and help overcome stress-related illness. Please do not delay taking this course as it might be for you as these students have expressed:

> *"The most profound thing that helped me change the quality of my life."*
> *"Every day is beautiful and life is really worth living since I learned Transformation Meditation."*
> *"There are no words that can express how glad I am that you have influenced my life!"*

For you to be completely reassured that you are spending your time and money wisely, we are so confident in the success of this course that we offer a full money-back guarantee. If for any reason you are not satisfied after the first class in the series, we will refund your money to you in full. It is important that you do not delay. Register for this class right away. For early registration we will give you a FREE additional class.

Thank you in advance for choosing us. We will make sure we do everything in our power to help you enjoy this program and obtain the maximum benefit from it. Please call or mail in your registration today in order to be sure to receive these special offers for early registration and to reserve your space. Learn to meditate. It will greatly enrich your life!

Sincerely,

Transformation Meditation
Foundation Series

Evening Classes
Tuesdays, Feb. 16 - March 9, or
March 23 - April 13, 7:30 PM - 9:00 PM

Morning Classes
Wednesdays, Feb. 17 - March 10, or Thurs.
March 25 - April 15, 10:30 AM - 12:00 PM

Studies of meditation have shown reduced stress and anxiety, lower blood pressure, reduced chronic pain, improved health, vitality and self esteem.

If you have never meditated or if you have tried and found it difficult to continue your practice, this course is for you. It will include the theory of meditation, effective techniques and practice time.

Meditation cannot be learned from a book or a tape. It requires an experienced teacher who can guide you in your progress.

(Your photo here)

(Your biography)

For more information call
(name and phone number)

Additional Benefits of Attending

Learn simple and effective ways to calm your mind and emotions and experience a state of inner peacefulness and well being.

Learn to increase your productivity & enjoyment of life.

Discover how to free yourself from disturbing thoughts and feelings and have harmonious relationships.

Some comments from students:

"I feel more peaceful and relaxed, yet I have greater energy and focus. My thinking is much clearer."

"My blood pressure dropped & my stress & anxiety were reduced. Everyday is beautiful and life is really worth living since I learned Transformational Meditation. I can never thank you enough."

" My chronic pain is gone and my insomnia & asthma have decreased greatly. Meditation is the single most profound thing that helped me change the quality of my life."

Location:

Your address, phone number and e-mail address

Tuition:
$75.00 for series of 4 classes and a 5th class Free with advance registration. Includes Manual.

Special - 5 more practice classes for just $55.00 - good for any practice classes on the schedule. (Save $20.00)
must be paid with series.

To register:

You can register for this class online by going to our website www._____ , or mail or hand in your check or credit card number.

Name_____

Address_____

_____zip code_____

Phone_____# people attending_____

Date of first class_____Ck amount_____

MCorVISA #_____Amt._____

Expiry date_____ Signature_____

Transformation Meditation Is for Everyone

Sherrie Wade, a Florida Licensed Mental Health Counselor and Board Certified Counselor, developed **Transformation Meditation.** It is an accumulation of twenty years of study of various meditation techniques at centers throughout the United States and India.

Transformation Meditation is a scientifically oriented practical application of meditation techniques. It includes the understanding of how the mind and body react to stress and how meditation philosophy and practice can be applied to everyday life to improve overall heath and productivity, and unfold inner peace.

Commonly Asked Questions

Q: How is Transformation Meditation different from other meditation techniques?

A: Transformation Meditation has its roots in the philosophy of yoga. Similar to other techniques, such as Transcendental Meditation, it utilizes mantra meditation techniques. Similar to Mindfulness Meditation, it also includes the ability to become the observer of your mind and actions. With the combination of these techniques, one gains the ability to understand and experience the state of meditation directly. This enhances one's ability to practice, accelerating the meditative experience.

Q: I have a difficult time concentrating, have too many thoughts in my head and find it hard to sit still. Can I learn to meditate? How long do I have to practice?

A: Most people have very active minds. The purpose of the mind is to think. How many thoughts you have in your mind is never a hindrance while practicing meditation. These techniques are designed to help improve your concentration and ability to relax. You will only practice for a few minutes at the beginning and develop your ability for longer sessions.

Q: How can meditation improve my health, lower blood pressure, and reduce chronic pain?

A: Meditation can improve your health by helping to strengthen your immune system. Your blood pressure can be lowered through the practice of meditation as your body's need for oxygen is reduced. Your heart doesn't have to work as hard and this can help normalize your blood pressure. Chronic pain can be reduced through increasing the body's natural pain-control chemicals such as seratonin and endorphins. It also allows you to transcend your body awareness as you do in deep sleep.

Q: Will Transformation Meditation conflict with my religious beliefs?

A: Transformation Meditation is a very scientific technique that creates a relaxation response. Many people find the practice and philosophy of meditation enhances their spirituality. People of all religious backgrounds are welcome and none of the techniques will interfere in any way with your religious beliefs or practices, but only enhance them.

Follow-up Letter

To be sent to prospective students

Date

Dear

It has been a while since you first called showing interest in the Transformation Meditation Course. We are wondering why we haven't heard from you. Are the times the classes are offered OK for you? Do you need more information about the course? Pleases call and let us know because we will gladly add additional classes for your convenience and give you all the information you need. If you are still unsure, call for a FREE individual meditation session to discuss your needs and learn more about how meditation can benefit you. We are confident that this course will benefit you greatly and we want to make sure that you do not miss this opportunity.

This course has helped many people and can help you in every area of your life. Meditation practice is an effective way to reduce stress and anxiety, improve concentration and focus, increase productivity, improve relationships and help overcome stress-related illness. Please do not delay taking this course as it might be for you as these students have expressed,

> *"The most profound thing that helped me change the quality of my life."*
> *"Everyday is beautiful and life is really worth living since I learned Transformation Meditation."*
> *"There are no words that can express how glad I am that you have influenced my life!"*

To make this an easy decision for you we even offer you a full money-back guarantee. If for any reason you are not satisfied after the first class in the series, we will refund your money to you in full. For early registration we will give you a FREE additional class and one free individual consultation.

We will make sure we do everything in our power to help you enjoy this program and obtain the maximum benefit from it. Please call or mail in your registration today in order to be sure to receive these special offers for early registration and to reserve your space. Learn to meditate, it will greatly enrich your life!

Sincerely,

Graduate Letter

To be sent to students towards the completion of the course

Date

As we move towards the completion of the Transformation Meditation Foundation Series, we want to express both our thanks and congratulations. Meditation is a continuous practice, always opening greater and greater levels of awareness, health and peaceful strength. We wholeheartedly invite you to continue your practice with us by registering for the ongoing meditation classes listed below. You can purchase tickets of classes, $75.00 for five or $120.00 for ten classes. Your tickets are good for any of these class times and classes do not have to be taken in a sequence. You may register in advance or at your first class.

Days	Times	Class Descriptions
Mondays	7:30PM - 9:00PM	**The Science of Meditation -** Learn more advanced meditation and breathing techniques and discuss the practical application of meditation philosophy in everyday life.
Tuesdays Thursdays	6:00PM - 7:30 PM or 12:15PM - 1:15PM	**Meditation Practice -** A relaxation and stress management group to help you practice. Learn new techniques and discuss the application of meditation.

The next Transformation Meditation Foundation Series starts Tuesday, March 4, at 7:30 PM and Thursday, March 6, at 10:00 AM, or you can attend a special Saturday two-session course on March 8 & 22, at 1:30 PM. Please tell your friends and family. If you have a friend or relative who registers for the class you can come with them and re-take this course for **Free** or receive one free intermediate class instead.

Sincerely,

Press Release for Community Calendar/Classes

To be sent to newspapers in your area that have a community calendar listing of local events or classes.

Date

Transformation Meditation Foundation Series for stress management, improved health and inner peace.

Classes start:

Tuesday, Dec. 1, 7:30 - 9:00 PM, series of 5 classes

Intermediate and advanced meditation classes
Study the philosophy and practice of meditation for Self-realization.

Ongoing classes Mondays 7:30 PM, Tuesdays 6 PM, Thursdays 12:15 & 7:30 PM.

For more information and registration call or write:

(Your name, address, phone number and e-mail address)

The following can be made into a poster size or overhead and used for your presentations along with your own students' comments.

Do you have any of these symptoms?

Feeling stressed out
Low energy
Trouble falling asleep
Anxiety
Panic attacks
Irrational fears
Unable to relax
Cardiovascular problems
High cholesterol
Phobias
Overweight

High blood pressure
Chronic pain
Chronic illness
Low mood
Low self-esteem
Unhappy
Low productivity
Excessive colds and flu
Unable to concentrate
Dependency on drugs or alcohol
Unhappy relationships

These may be due to or worsened by excessive stress!

10 ways recent research shows that you can benefit from meditation and relaxation training

- Reduce Stress and Anxiety
- Learn to Relax
- Help in the Healing of Chronic Illness and Pain
- Overcome Panic Attacks and Phobias
- Find Out How To Take Charge of Your Life, Maximize Your Abilities
- Develop a Healthy Sense of Self-Esteem and Self-Love
- Reconnect To Your Spiritual Self
- Help to Overcome Destructive Fears and Emotions
- Find Balance, Feel Great and Perform Better
- Live longer, Enjoy Your Life and Be Happy

These are just a few of the comments from former students

"*Sherrie taught me how to meditate a year ago and since that time it's become an indispensable part of my life. I gained so much from it. I have a serious illness and one of the benefits I've gotten is that by meditating I am able to handle chronic pain without the use of pain killers. I know that without meditation I would be at best suffering severely. In my opinion Sherrie's approach to teaching meditation techniques makes it possible for anyone who is interested to learn meditation. I just think she is great and I can't thank her enough.*" P.L., Boca Raton

"*I feel like I can handle things on my own, thanks to you and your unending support. I truly believe you are the most aware person I've met and I mean that sincerely. Thank you from the bottom of my heart.*" H.F., Coral Springs

Newspaper Column

"Positive Solutions" published in *Happy Times Monthly*

Having your own column in a local newspaper can be a good way for you to share this knowledge and for you to receive recognition and help to promote your classes. The following are questions and answers from Sherrie Wade's column published in Boca Raton, FL, October 1999 - January 2001.

This will give you insight into how to write your own column for your local newspaper. It will also help you to answer some of the common questions that your students may ask.

Q.: I have heard that meditation is important for health and a balanced lifestyle. If I meditate will I develop a complacent attitude about life and not care about things or feel for people?

A.: Meditation gives you more energy, insight and a sense of well being, Oneness and love for all people. It is not like a drug or narcotic that anesthetizes you to life. You will have a full range of emotions but can free yourself from the useless waste of energy caused by fears, anger or anxieties that hinder you from enjoying each precious moment of life.

Q.: I have a hard time understanding how the being is immortal and may even reincarnate into another body. I experience myself as being mortal and, like everyone else who has walked the earth, I will die. How can I grasp this idea?

A.: The physical body is made up of five elements: earth, water, air, fire and space. When it dies it will change form and go back into earth and space. Science teaches us that energy can never be destroyed. Therefore, even on the physical level you will continue. On the spiritual level you are pure energy or space and that never changes. Whether you believe it takes on another form or not is your personal choice; however, you can directly experience the Pure Consciousness that you are in meditation.

Q.: I have been meditating and practicing positive thinking for five years. I feel like I got it but then I lose it. Sometimes I feel happy and connected with my inner Self which is peaceful, but at other times I am totally cßaught up again. Then I start to doubt if what I am doing is working at all. Am I doing something wrong?

A.: What you are describing is a common experience. As you progress you are getting clearer, but sometimes you slip back into old thinking patterns and belief systems. This happens because these patterns which took a long time to form take time to dissolve. Just remind yourself of the times that you felt connected. Even when you forget, it is a kind of remembering because you are aware that you are not relaxed and you can change it. If you keep doing your practice you will be able to maintain that higher state more and more in your life and dissolve these old patterns.

Q.: My husband makes a good living, yet it always seems that we are short of money and struggling to pay our bills. We seem to always live beyond our means. How can we stop this bad habit?

A.: Someone who makes very little but lives simply may never feel that they have financial problems. Someone who makes a lot may always feel burdened by finances. If you want to feel easy and free you have to learn to live within your means. Your satisfaction should come from the joy within your own heart and not just from material things. These things never bring lasting happiness. When you find the happiness within, then you are freed from needing so many things. In fact, you will find that life is even more enjoyable with less to pay for, take care of and protect.

Q.: My parents are very negative and fearful people. When I am with my friends I am fine, but when I am around them I start to think negative and destructive thoughts. What can I do?

A.: The company that you keep has a definite effect on you. You can excuse yourself from their company or else work on keeping the thought in your head positive and free. It will be much easier for you if you stop trying to change them and instead accept them as being perfect the way they are. You can repeat a mantra or positive affirmation silently to yourself. When you don't like the show on TV you change the station with the remote. When you don't like the thought in your head or the company, just switch it!

Q.: I know that meditation is important and good for me but I never seem to make the time to do it. Why is that and what can I do?

A:. Many people ask, why is it that when something is good for me I don't do it? You have habituated yourself in a certain way and now want to change that. The quickest way to do this is to find the company that is participating in activities that will reinforce your new behavior. If you go to a meditation group regularly or, similarly, if you work out in the gym or take yoga classes regularly, then you will develop this new positive lifestyle change. Company is stronger than will power, so find good company!

Q.: Why is it so much more difficult for me to meditate at home than with a group?

A.: It is hard for you to meditate at home because your habit patterns and environment are not yet that conducive for meditation. It isn't hard for you to brush your teeth because you have the toothpaste and brush prepared near the sink and you do it every day. You can create a place where you can sit everyday with nice things such as pictures, candles and flowers. You can also read spiritually uplifting and enlightening books and writings; or you can listen to meditation recordings that will assist in your meditation. Then you will have more of a meditative environment in your home. Group meditation is more powerful because you are away from distractions and you benefit from the energy of many people meditating together. Therefore, it is important to do both.

Q.: I have tried so hard not to think negative thoughts and to change them to positive ones. No matter how hard I try, my mind just keeps generating negative thoughts and worries. What should I do?

A.: The nature of the mind is that it is filled with thoughts both negative and positive, as well as worries, concerns and joys. You don't think that your eyes should stop seeing whatever they see or your ears shouldn't hear. Why do you think that your mind shouldn't think thoughts? The thoughts in your mind will not be a problem to you when you pause and ask yourself: who is it that is thinking these thoughts? Then you will get in touch with the Knower or observer of your thoughts. When you observe your thoughts you become aware that they are just passing waves of perception. They have no power over you the observer unless you give them meaning and believe them. You will gain the power to let go of those thoughts that aren't useful and bring in the thoughts that are helpful. You have then become the master of your own mind.

Q.: My mind is always so active and filled with thoughts, worries and concerns. How can I ever achieve peace of mind?

A.: There is no such thing as peace of mind. The very nature of the mind is to generate thoughts. Sometimes the thoughts are more turbulent and sometimes more peaceful. The job of the mind is to churn thoughts. Therefore, if you try to find peace on the level of your mind you will fail. Instead, you need to become aware of the peace that is always there. The very one who can observe or watch the mind is always peaceful. Therefore, if you shift your attention away from your mind to the observer or Knower of your mind, you will be at peace.

Q.: I think I may be using meditation to escape my problems or to hide from my life. Is that possible?

A.: That is a totally incorrect understanding. You have to meditate in order to have a good life. When meditating you are becoming strong; then you can deal with everything much more effectively and efficiently. One is so used to using only the mind to solve problems, but the mind is very limited. When you meditate you open up to a more expansive view and then your ability greatly increases. You can become healthy, happy and live in a state of freedom and fulfillment.

Q.: How can I handle memories from the past that make me feel sad while meditating?

A.: What is a memory? It is a group of thoughts, images or feelings regarding some events that you believe happened in the past. If they are good you feel happy; if bad, you feel sad. Is there anything you can do to change the past? Have you changed from the moment before you had these thoughts or memories? You are the same person. The mind is always fluctuating and changing and the memory is only occurring in your mind. If you focus on the You that hasn't changed, you can create good memories for the future.

Q.: I have read that being attached to material things and to people leads to suffering. How can one not be attached when we enjoy and depend on so many things and people in our lives?

A.: Yes, we depend on things and people for our enjoyment and ease in living and there is nothing wrong with this. The problem comes when you think that these things will make you permanently happy. Then you either need more of them or fear you will lose them. Therefore, one has to dig the source of inner happiness and joy which can't be taken away from you. The things, people and situations will always change. Even in the most perfect marriage someone usually dies first. Therefore, to be free of attachment, you have to know your inner being that is always peaceful, because it is unchanging.

Q.: I have been trying to meditate for a number of years but always get frustrated and can't do it. What should I do?

A.: First, I recommend that you find a teacher and a group to meditate with. Also doing some yoga or breathing techniques first will make it much easier. With proper instruction and preparation meditation is easy. Meditation is a state of awareness of your own true nature. Whenever you notice the space between your thoughts or at the back of your thoughts and when you put your attention on the Knower or observer of your thoughts, you will experience your original state which is always present and forever peaceful.

Q.: I am in pain over a breakup of a relationship. Even though I know this is not the right person for me, and that we need to end it, I am still suffering over the loss. What should I do?

A.: When you think you have gained something you will always suffer when it is lost. The work then is on your own inner sense of fulfillment. This requires practice because the human system will always suffer when loss occurs. This is not your fault, it is made that way. Gaining the awareness that you are fulfilled within yourself will help, because, once you have that, it will always be with you. Through practicing living in this fulfilled state you can remain free from the suffering of the body and the mind.

Q.: I can be feeling fine and then all of a sudden worries come into my head and I get very upset thinking these things. I try to think other things but it just doesn't work. What else can I do?

A.: If these worries were in someone else's head they wouldn't have an effect on you. If you were watching a movie concerning a similar drama of what you are thinking, and it was happening to an actor on the stage, you might even enjoy the show. Through the practice of meditation you can learn how to de-identify with these destructive thoughts or worries. Then you will experience the same peace that you were knowing before the thoughts arose.

Transformation Meditation Online Institute
Our Home-Study Courses

Certificates of Achievements are awarded upon completion of any of our courses. (continuing education clock hours where applicable)

Transformation Meditation Teacher Training, by Shree

Doubt Free Meditation Foundation Series, by Shree

Stillness of Breath: Praanaayaam for Meditators, by Brijendra

Essence of Patanjali Yog Sootras, by Brijendra

Essence of the Bhagavad Gita, by Glen Kezwer

Advanced Certificate in Meditation Teaching and Yogic Science

Awarded after completion of four of our home study-courses and one year of listening to our satsang podcasts. You will then be awarded this advanced certificate.

Become a Transformation Meditation Center Service Provider

When three or more of your center's teachers complete our *Home-study Teacher Training Course,* a certificate to frame and display at your Center will be provided and you will receive all the benefits of this program.

On-Line Registration:

To register by credit card or electronic check over a secure connection, visit our website at: **http://www.transformedu.com** and click on the registration button at the top of the page. A confirmation email of your order will be sent to you.

For more information, email info@transformationmeditation.com

97452580R00102

Made in the USA
Columbia, SC
15 June 2018